D0909986

HARVEST

"I've been able to get to know the 'behind the scene' Stacy Lyn Harris. Unlike many other TV personalities, she is the same person off-camera as she is when she is entertaining our viewers with her endearing **Southern charm and culinary expertise**. From the moment I took my first bite of her Venison Scaloppine, I was hooked on Stacy for life.

This book captures the essence of Stacy Lyn Harris' **sustainable lifestyle, devotion to her faith and family and true love of incredible, yet uncomplicated cuisine**. Although Stacy's kitchen is decidedly Southern, **her recipes appeal to anyone who appreciates great seasonal food that is locally sourced**. She has inspired me to plant more, grow more and enjoy life more than ever before.

Our television crew can't wait for our next visit to the Harris kitchen. Once the cameras are turned off, the dishes she just prepared are consumed in a veritable feeding frenzy. Take it from someone who has had the distinct pleasure of eating dozens of Stacy Lyn Harris' brand of cooking anything with fur, fins and feathers, **she is the real deal**. This is a book that you and your family will cherish for years to come."

— Scott Leysath, host of the award winning show *The Sporting Chef* and best selling author

Stacy Lyn's Harvest Cookbook

The New Recipes & Tips for Sustainable Living

Cook Fresh Food Every Day of the Year

Stacy Lyn Harris

STACY LYN'S HARVEST COOKBOOK.

First Edition

Harcover ISBN: 978-0-9838799-3-0

1. Cooking 2. Seasonal 3. Vegetables 4. Wild Game 5. Southern

6. Farm Produce

I. Harris, Stacy Lyn II. Title

Stacy Lyn's HARVEST Cookbook may be purchased at special quantity discounts to use as corporate premiums, sales promotions, corporate training programs, gifts, fund raising, book clubs, or educational purposes for schools and universities. For more information contact stacylynharris@gmail.com.

www.stacylynharris.com
Printed in China

Publisher:

Gray Forest Publishing, LLC

Pike Road, Alabama 36064

Photography: Stacy Lyn Harris and Graylyn Harris

Cover Design and Layout : Lynne Hopwood

Design Collaboration: Lynne Hopwood, Stacy Lyn Harris, and Graylyn Harris

Also by Stacy Lyn Harris

Happy Healthy Family Tracking the Outdoors In

Introduction

My grandmother's words, "Food is more than just something to eat; relationships 'stick' when built around a table of good quality fresh food," are just as clear in my mind today as when she said them to me. Every time I open a new can of homemade pickles to eat alongside that egg salad sandwich made with fresh from the chicken eggs, or open that perfect jar of relish to top my fresh black-eyed peas, I am brought back to my grandmother's house and her simple, beautiful way of living life.

In my pursuit of creating a beautiful life and flavorful nutritious food for my family, most of my days are spent in the garden and kitchen with my children. In my opinion, education about life, science, math, history, design, and art begin in the garden, kitchen, and at family table. The natural curiosity from watching vegetables grow from a seed rallies all kinds of conversational and learning moments. Each one of these conversations leads to another and then another.

The kids all have a part in the process of harvesting food for the table whether it be picking fruit and vegetables from the farmer's market, planning our own garden and harvesting it, or saving seeds for next year's garden. We have not forced our children to work with us in planting and harvesting the garden; quite the opposite. They feel that they are missing out on the fun if they aren't with us. Our relationships continue to deepen as we work and then as we share the bounty at the dinner table together.

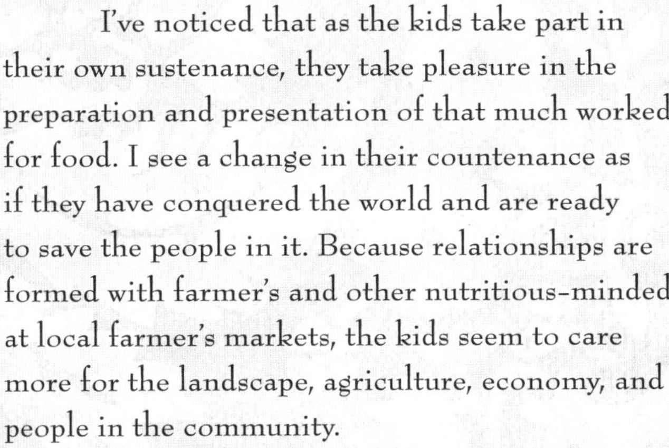

I've noticed that as the kids take part in their own sustenance, they take pleasure in the preparation and presentation of that much worked for food. I see a change in their countenance as if they have conquered the world and are ready to save the people in it. Because relationships are formed with farmer's and other nutritious-minded at local farmer's markets, the kids seem to care more for the landscape, agriculture, economy, and people in the community.

Family and community relationships become stronger when everyone is working toward the same end and discovering new ideas and concepts together. In the life of a gardener, one never stops learning and sharing. Father teaching son, and in our case, at times, son teaching mom; grandfather teaching grandson; and brother teaching sister. It doesn't stop there. In our family, instead of passing down silver and gold, we pass down heirloom seeds that have been in the family for generations.

How awesome it has been to have my grandmother's recipes, and cherished are her heirloom seeds saved and passed down from proliferous plants. Talk about LEGACY! I have the seeds from the direct plants she used to prepare the recipes she graciously put on the table and I have the recipe box containing the treasured recipes.

Historically, just about every home had a kitchen garden and a few chickens in the back yard, if not out of necessity, merely for the pleasure of raising nutritious food for their families. As our lives have gotten busier and space increasingly sparse, people have relied on supermarkets for their food source. I'm not saying that supermarkets are bad; I love their convenience just like everyone else, but I am saying there's more…Local foods are splendid, local farmer's are worth knowing, and growing food brings pleasure that only those that do it can explain.

I am still, like a fascinated child, in awe each time that I plant a seed and see it grow from a seedling to a full grown plant producing nourishment for my family. At times, I have lived in very small urban spaces and felt unconnected to the sources of my food. By planting a few herbs in the window sill or a vertical Italian pot on the back porch, I was able to fulfill that need. Many folks only need to know the farmer's who grow their food. They automatically feel the connection to their food sources by connecting to the farmer who grows it.

I find that people want to grow their own food, but feel incredibly overwhelmed with all the "time, energy, and knowledge that it will take that they don't think they have!" Believe me, I totally get that. I was the same way. Why not let the experts grow the food? It used to be that most everyone was an expert in growing their own food. You can be too. It's really just a matter of getting good seeds, putting them into good soil, watering and nourishing it, and waiting. That's it! It's just that SIMPLE! and Oh, so fulfilling.

If any of you know me, you know about my family's Southern tradition of fishing and hunting for most our protein; the rest we outsource from local farmers. My husband, Scott, has always been a "Daniel Boone" of sorts. His life begins and ends with the outdoors, and he is a very self-sufficient type of guy. During our marriage, he has rubbed off on me a great deal. I see

many of these traits in my kids and it brings me joy to know that they will "figure" things out!

Hunting is just a way of life for us here in the South. It wouldn't be strange at all to show up on Christmas Day to find that my dad was in the woods getting a hunt in before the festivities. As I've gotten older and having married a hunter, I see the benefits of eating free-range organic meats. Growing up, I didn't like the taste of "wild foods" very much. Once I married and became the principal cook for my family, mainly for a husband that filled the freezer full of free-range meats, I came to realize after much experimentation, that free-range and pasture-fed meats are packed full of flavor; you just have to know how to cook it.

That's when I pulled out the ancient recipes from my ancestors whose only sources of protein, besides fish, were free-range and pasture-fed. Wanting to please my husband and cook what he harvested and wanting to please my pallet, I poured myself into understanding how to cook like the greats. It clicked in my mind that you simply had to pair the right cut of meat with the right cooking method. It's really that simple - one of the reasons I am writing this book is to make life more simple, flavorful, and beautiful for you to live.

As I realized how amazing the flavors of fresh vegetables, fruits, eggs, free-range, and pasture-fed meats could

be, I never turned back. The nutritional value alone is worth eating fresh and local, not to mention it's sustainability. The vegetables have been allowed to ripen on the vine and free-range meats are consistently lower in fat and cholesterol, and higher in vitamins B, zinc, niacin, and phosphorus as well as Omega 3 fatty acids.

This book has been a true pleasure to write. Throughout the book I have given tips for growing certain fruits and vegetables as well as preserving them. There are many, many "how to's" from making your own sausage to saving the seeds of your best producing tomatoes to produce even better ones the next year.

I would take great pleasure in knowing that you ordered a packet of heirloom seeds, saved them, planted them the following year and years after that and passed them down to all of your children and then to their children.

Even if you don't put any of the gardening to practice, you will know how to at the end of reading this book. I'm proud of the recipes and hope that you will cook to your hearts delight and make these recipes your own passing your favorite ones down throughout generations. I find it a privilege to share with you my life and hope you are truly blessed by the words, thoughts, tips, and recipes in the words of this book.

John 4: 35...Behold, I say unto you, Lift up your eyes, and look on the fields; for they are white already to HARVEST.

www.StacyLynHarris.com

Contents

The Garden

History has given us many gifts, one of which is the continuation of plants using seeds dating back thousands of years. I love just dreaming of the life our ancestors lived and the gardens that they tended and nurtured. My family of nine makes a habit of visiting historic plantations in different states each year. The one commonality is that they all have a garden spot, whether it be a knot garden, square foot garden, or a huge planted garden. I love them all as I am sure their owner's have through the years.

More than the historical romanticism that I love so dearly, heirloom gardening affords very practical benefits. Many of the best tasting, most prolific, healthy, and health producing plants are harvested from heirloom seeds. Additionally, family unity and sustainability as well as being part of history, geography, science, and wild life contribute to an abundance of living and fulfillment that very few activities can match.

Heirloom varieties are usually not as uniform in shape as hybrid plants, but the flavor is exceptional in comparison. We are used to seeing beautiful, perfect-looking specimens in the grocery store, therefore they appear to be less attractive, but once you have tasted the modestly captivating heirloom variety, they become alluringly gorgeous because of what thy contribute in flavor, texture, and their extraordinary uniqueness.

Because heirlooms have not been genetically modified, they are able to produce plants that are just as prolific, healthy, disease resistant, and resilient to weather extremes as they did for our ancestors. Genetically modified plants have genes added or deleted from them causing alterations in the entire structure of the plant. Genetic engineering is usually done to achieve a trait that is not normally held by an organism. These genetically modified plants bear sterile seeds or seeds that revert only to one of the parent genes, therefore never producing the same plant if producing a plant at all. Heirloom seeds are open-pollinating seeds, which mean that they can reproduce themselves from seeds. God created the cycle of plant life whereby a seed falls to the ground and the seed produces another plant in its likeness. Why disturb the perfect means of reproduction given by our Creator?

It is truly amazing that by planting heirloom seeds, we are planting a piece of history. Our own native Indians have provided us with the original corn, squash, and potatoes that they survived on. Many seeds traveled over the seas and were brought by European, and Asian immigrants. The Europeans brought cabbage, pole beans, and carrots. The Asians brought radishes, lettuces, and onions. We are tasting the same flavors and textures as did our predecessors. History is being seen right in our flourishing heirloom gardens.

Family stories are connected to many of the heirloom seeds we possess. The seeds, just like the infamous family recipes, get passed down through the generations along with the stories of our great-great grandmothers and grandfathers that harvested and cooked from these very plants and relied on them for their sustenance. My dad is passing the purple-hull peas that have adorned our table for as long as I remember down to me and my children. I am sure that our ancestors enjoyed family unity as I do with my children in the great outdoors actually living life while sharing responsibility and passing down life giving truths by teaching the necessities of life while working along side of one another. These "real" activities of life give competence to the next generation and teach responsibility and care for the earth.

Heirloom seeds consistently yield a crop of fruits, vegetables, and herbs with extra-ordinary flavor, life giving health, family unity, and life long sustainability. Our ancestors have always relied on their kitchen gardens as a way of life and we should learn to do the same and pass down our knowledge and passion for generations to come. I look forward to passing down my favorite life giving heirloom seeds and recipes to my children and children's children as well as to anyone else who will appreciate them.

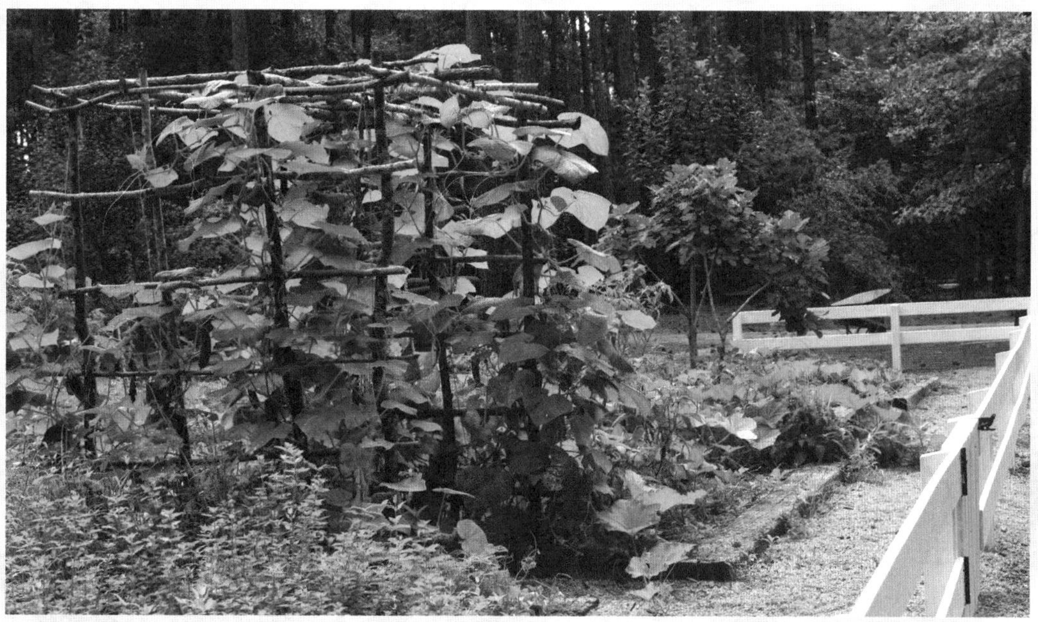

Strawberry Almond Clafoutis is fantastic for Sunday or Mother's Day Brunch. You can prepare this dish in less than 5 minutes and leave the work to the oven for the rest of the cooking time. There aren't many dishes that I can say that about!

The first time I made this dish, I was in love! I remember walking in the my herb garden one sunny Sunday afternoon looking at the light hitting the juicy fresh strawberries.

I had just read about this delicious dessert and remembered that it looked really very simple. I gathered up my strawberries and prepared this lovely dish in what seemed like no time at all.

Clafoutis is a baked French dessert originating in France during the 19th century. Traditionally black cherries were used in this dish, but other fruit substitutions are equally as wonderful.

To make clafoutis, the fruit of choice is arranged in a buttered dish with a cross between flan and a pancake-like batter poured over the top of the fruit and baked. It is simple, yet ever so tasty and gorgeous. I have used pears, peaches, blackberries, raspberries, and cranberries before, and every time I end up with an amazing dish.

Strawberry Almond Clafoutis

Serves 6

½ tablespoon butter
1 pound strawberries, hulled and halved (about 2 cups)
2 teaspoons cornstarch
1¼ cup milk
1 cup sugar, plus extra for sprinkling
3 large eggs
1 tablespoon vanilla or almond extract (I like almond)
½ teaspoon salt
1 cup flour
½ cup sliced almonds
powdered sugar, for garnish

Preheat oven to 350 degrees F. Grease a 2-quart baking dish with the butter and sprinkle with a little sugar. Toss strawberries in the cornstarch and arrange berries, cut side down, in the baking dish.

Using a blender, mix the milk, sugar, eggs, almond extract, salt, and flour for about 15 seconds. Pour batter over the strawberries. Sprinkle almonds over the top of mixture.

Bake in preheated oven for 45 to 60 minutes or until puffed, golden brown, and set in the center. Sprinkle with powdered sugar and serve warm.

Strawberries are full of antioxidants and vitamins! If you had to choose just one fruit to grow, this is the one!

Squash Boats

Serves 4

I love to eat these jewels as a meal in the summertime. This dish is light and refreshing after a long day in our hot, Alabama summers. It is also hearty and tasty enough to leave me satisfied.

Ingredients

4 yellow squash
3 tablespoons olive oil, divided
1 Vidalia onion, chopped
3 cloves garlic, chopped
2 tomatoes, chopped
1 teaspoon oregano, chopped
1 teaspoon basil, chopped
¾ cup bread crumbs, divided
1½ cup Parmesan cheese, divided
1 teaspoon Kosher salt
½ teaspoon freshly ground pepper
2 eggs, beaten
4 tablespoons butter
2 tablespoons parsley, for garnish

Preheat oven to 350 degrees.

Half squash lengthwise and scoop out the seeds and soft flesh with a spoon and discard. Place squash into a baking dish.

Heat 2 tablespoons of olive oil in a sauté pan over medium heat and sauté onions and garlic for about 5 minutes or until onions are translucent. Remove from heat. Add tomatoes and cook 2 minutes. Add ¼ cup bread crumbs, ¾ cup cheese, salt, pepper, and the eggs into the skillet and mix well.

Mound the stuffing into the cavity of the squash. Top the mounds with remaining bread crumbs and dot each with butter. Bake for 20 minutes then remove the pan and sprinkle the remaining Parmesan cheese over the top of the squash and return to the oven for another 10 minutes or until mounds are golden brown and squash can be punctured easily with a fork.

Remove from oven and drizzle with remaining olive oil and garnish with basil and parsley.

Fried Squash *with* Tomato *and* Pesto

Serves 4

This is a fantastic meal for those days your garden harvest is packed full of squash. If you have some frozen pesto on hand, this is an especially quick and easy meal. I prefer to use my left-over tomato sauce from my meatless spaghetti in preparation for this recipe. This is also a great dish when entertaining because you can prepare the pesto and tomato sauce in advance and refrigerate for later usage. This dish is amazingly impressive in appearance and taste! You can substitute eggplant for squash in this recipe.

Ingredients

1 cup Basic Tomato Sauce (page 42)
1 cup Basil Pesto (page 113)
4 medium sized squash
1 cup flour
1 teaspoon kosher salt
½ teaspoon pepper
2 eggs
1 tablespoon water
1 cup bread crumbs
Olive oil, for frying
4 tablespoons butter, for frying
2 tomatoes, sliced into ¼ inch slices
Basil leaves, for garnishing

Prepare tomato sauce and pesto.

Cut squash into ¼" slices lengthwise.

On a large plate, mix flour, salt, and pepper. On a second plate beat eggs and water together. Place bread crumbs on a third plate. Coat squash slices into seasoned flour, then egg mixture, then bread crumbs.

In a hot sauté pan, mix butter and oil. When sizzling, place coated slices in pan for about 2 to 3 minutes per side or until squash is tender. Cook in batches. Transfer to a platter and keep warm.

Place tablespoon of pesto in center of a plate and begin to layer fried squash, tomato sauce, tomato, and repeat beginning again with the pesto until you have at least 4 slices of squash. Garnish with a basil leaf.

Figs

Figs,

It is amazing how food evokes such memories. My first and most precious remembrance of figs is eating them while sitting in the top of my Granny's fig tree right after doing flips off the bars holding up her clothes line. Every year she would cut the tree right to the ground and I would be shocked in the spring to see it growing into another tree. By the end of the summer, it was larger than the year before.

Fig trees have been mentioned from the days of Adam and Eve (Genesis 3:7). Throughout the ages figs have been a daily staple for the Hebrews, Egyptians, Cretans, and Romans. Figs are one of the Israelites top 7 traditional foods and have always symbolized wealth and prosperity in their culture. The Spaniards brought this amazing fruit to America in the 1600's and it remains today as one of the world's healthiest ingredients.

Both the fruit and the leaves hold healing and preventative powers. The fruit, fresh or dried, contains one of the highest amounts of fiber aiding in weight loss and post-menapausal breast cancer as well as having a high percentage of potassium which helps control blood pressure. The leaves are known to contain anti-diabetic properties that will reduce the amount of insulin diabetic patients require. The leaves have also been known to slow cancer cells considerably.

Figs pair beautifully with meats, especially that of quail and fish. I love to serve fish steamed in a fig leaf with various herbs. Figs are extremely perishable and need to be eaten within a day of picking or purchasing. If you have figs available, take the opportunity to dry any unused fig (page 129) and eat them as a snack or rehydrate them when you are ready to cook with them.

Fig Bread

Yields 1 Loaf

This bread is a favorite in my family. My little ones love mashing up the figs and I love having their helping hands in the kitchen. The reward of eating this yummy, sweet bread isn't that bad either.

Ingredients

2 cups all purpose flour
1 ½ teaspoons baking soda
½ teaspoons salt
2 large eggs
½ teaspoon vanilla extract
½ cup butter room temperature, plus more for preparing pan
1 cup sugar, plus 3 tablespoons for seasoning pan
1 cup ripe figs
½ cup chopped pecans

Preheat oven to 350 degrees.

Stir the flour, baking soda and salt into a medium bowl and set aside.

In a separate bowl, whisk the eggs and vanilla extract together and set aside.

Butter a 9x5x3inch loaf pan. Sprinkle 3 tablespoons of sugar in the bottom of the pan. Set aside.

In a large bowl use an electric hand mixer to cream the butter and sugar until light and fluffy. Slowly pour the egg mixture into the butter while mixing continuously.

Mix dry ingredients into the batter until just incorporated.

Mash figs with a fork so that they still have texture. Add figs to the mixture. Fold in the nuts. Pour the batter into pan. Bake for 1 hour and 15 minutes or until toothpick comes out clean.

Cool the bread on a wire rack for 10 minutes. Slice and serve.

Figs Stuffed with Mascarpone and Maple Walnuts

Serves 6 to 8

Figs are luscious served savory or sweet. There seems to be a magical quality about this amazing adaptable fruit. When stuffed with mascarpone, the dish becomes velvety and then the crunch of the maple walnuts makes this dish sing.

Ingredients

16 figs
4 ounces cream cheese
4 ounces mascarpone cheese
1 tablespoon parsley, chopped
1 tablespoon honey, plus more for drizzling
1 ounces (¼ cup) chopped walnuts
Maple Walnuts (page 65)

Preheat oven to 350 degrees.

Cross the top half of the figs with a paring knife, dividing the stem base into fourths.

Mix cream cheese, mascarpone, parsley, honey, and 1 ounce of walnuts in a medium bowl until smooth. Stuff about a teaspoon of the mixture into each fig. Place figs on cookie sheet and bake for about 10 minutes.

Prepare maple walnuts. Drizzle with honey and serve warm.

Composting, Making Black Gold in the Back Yard

Composting not only improves the soil but reduces waste, not to mention saves money on fertilizer. The only requirement to composting is to have a special receptacle to discard certain types of kitchen wastes, such as fruit and vegetable peels, dead leaves and grasses or remnants from a spent garden. This is great for our family in that trash builds up quite fast with a house of 9. These receptacles can range from a container on the kitchen counter filled with the appropriate kitchen scraps all the way to a large professional composting bin. Composting can be accomplished through several inexpensive methods from worm composting, composting tumblers that you purchase at your local garden store, or a backyard composting structure. Compost is naturally degraded, creating healthy fertilizer and mulching material that can be used in your lawn or garden.

To begin composting simply place a layer of about 6 inches of green ingredients (kitchen waste, hair, garden waste, grass clippings) in the bottom of your receptacle, soak with water, then layer about 2 inches of brown ingredients (wood chips, straw, dry leaves, sawdust), then continue to layer and turn periodically. To speed the process of composting you can add an activator which can also be purchased at your garden store. As your gardens grow, the

need for more compost is important in putting nourishment back into the ground. Green material is high in nitrogen and the brown material is high in carbon.

The boys built a double bin this year for our growing garden. They use one side for composting and the other for dressing deer. Multiple deer carcasses can become mulch within a few months and will add incredible minerals, nutrients, and beneficial bacteria to the soil.

Tomatoes

Tomatoes, Quintessential Summer

To say that "our family loves tomatoes" is an understatement. We love to can, dry, freeze them; eat them in sauces, on pasta, salads, and especially eat the fabulously simple tomato sandwich. Tomatoes make everything taste great. It is a crazy thing that these tasty creations were once considered poisonous by Europeans! Boy, did they ever miss out!

Each year we have been planting different heirloom varieties and having a family taste test to judge which variety is best. We have planted Chocolate Stripe, Brandywine, Bonnie's Best, Paste tomatoes, and several cherry tomato varieties. The all around favorite was Bonnie's Best tomato. Bonnie's Best Heirloom was created at the turn of the century in Union Springs, Alabama. Although Bonnie's Best won, all of them have winning qualities. For instance, the Chocolate Stripe is incredibly beautiful adorned with green and red stripes vertically around the entire tomato and the Brandywine is succulently sweet and juicy. We plan on crossing a few generations of these tomato plants and experimenting with making our own variety.

Saving Tomato Seeds

Saving seeds from tomatoes is a little different than saving seeds from most vegetables. It is not hard at all, only a little more time consuming, but VERY worth it. I like to save seeds from at least 3 tomatoes from each variety. You'll need to do each of the following steps separately for each variety. Our family of 9 needs about 100 tomato plants to have canned tomatoes throughout the winter, therefore we save at least 100 seeds.

1. Harvest seeds from your favorite healthiest tomato plant.
2. Cut the fruit in half. Squeeze the seeds into a clean container. Double the volume of liquid by adding equal parts pure water.
3. Let the tomatoes ferment in a warm, far away place (they stink!) for 3 days or until a scum form on the top. Add more water and stir.
4. Pour water off of the top discarding the seeds that float. The good seeds will drop to the bottom of the container. Repeat until only good seeds remain.
5. Transfer seeds into a strainer and dry with a towel. Place seeds on a clean plate until completely dry.
6. Store seeds in a small glass jar in a cool, dark place.

Even though there has been controversy as to the category that tomatoes belong, whether fruit or vegetable, the Supreme Court ruled that tomatoes are a vegetable for import purposes.

Growing up in the South, most everyone would try their hand at growing tomatoes. My dad would always say, "Anyone can grow a tomato." Of course, he has the greenest thumbs of just about anyone I know. I do not think I ever ate in the summertime at my Granny's house without the presence of fried green tomatoes accompanying my meal.

Fried green tomatoes have grown in status all over the country as of late, and rightly so. Their mild tartness and crunch lends them to a variety of dishes. Most of us in the South have always had them alongside a full plate of meat, butter beans, mashed potatoes, and any other seasonal vegetables with a piece of buttery cornbread. Recently, chefs everywhere are seeing the enormous potential of the fried green tomatoes and green tomatoes in general.

One of the nice things about frying green tomatoes is that you can salvage the imperfect tomatoes if they are large enough to get enough surface area for frying. I like to get these tomatoes at the end of the season when the vines are nearing the end of productivity and the tomatoes are likely not to ripen properly.

If you are shopping for green tomatoes to use for frying, be sure to choose firm tomatoes. The variety is not as important as the firmness of the tomato. Any good beefsteak brings good results. If you are gathering them from your garden, again choose fully grown firm tomatoes.

I have written two recipes for Fried Green Tomatoes. They are both extremely wonderful, but the baked version has ⅓ less calories and fat than the fried version. I just couldn't choose which one to put in the book, so I chose both!

Whichever you choose to make, they go great on hamburgers or as a side for hamburgers or a slab of ribs. I like them as a stand-alone meal!!

Original Fried Green Tomatoes

Ingredients

4 large firm green tomatoes
1 cup all-purpose flour
1 teaspoon salt, more for sprinkling
½ teaspoon pepper
2 eggs
1 tablespoon water
1 cup bread crumbs
1 cup olive oil for frying
4 tablespoons butter

Slice the tomatoes ¼ inch thick.

On a large plate, mix flour, salt, and pepper. On a second plate beat eggs and water together. Place bread crumbs on a third plate. Coat tomato slices into seasoned flour, then egg mixture, then bread crumbs.

In a hot sauté pan, mix butter and oil. When sizzling, place coated slices in pan for about 2 to 3 minutes per side or until tomatoes are tender. Cook in batches and add more oil if needed. Transfer to a platter, sprinkle with extra salt and serve warm.

Healthier Crunchier "Baked" Fried Green Tomatoes

Ingredients

4 large firm green tomatoes
1½ cup all purpose flour
1 teaspoon Kosher salt, more for sprinkling
½ teaspoon pepper
1 cup plain greek yogurt
½ cup buttermilk
1½ cup Panko Bread Crumbs
Pam Cooking Spray or olive oil for drizzling

Slice tomatoes ⅛ inch thick.

On a large plate mix flour, salt, and pepper. Place yogurt and buttermilk on a second plate, and Panko Bread Crumbs on a third plate. Coat tomatoes with the flour mixture, then the yogurt - buttermilk mixture (you may want to put the yogurt in a small bowl so that dipping them is easier), then the Panko Bread Brumbs.

Place coated tomatoes on a cookie sheet and spray with Pam Cooking Spray liberally on both sides or drizzle them on both sides with olive oil. Bake in a 350 degree oven for about 7 minutes on one side then flip them over and bake for another 5 to 7 minutes.

Transfer to a platter, sprinkle with extra salt and serve warm.

Tomato Pie

Serves 8

I have fond memories of this pie. My grandfather had 4 brothers and 1 sister that were very close. Every year they and their children and grandchildren would meet at Orange Beach, Alabama where my great aunts would cook massive amounts of food. Amazingly, one of my favorite dishes was Tomato Pie. Once you try it, you'll understand why!

Ingredients

1 homemade pie crust (page 43)
3 tablespoons mayonnaise
¾ cup dry breadcrumbs
2½ pounds heirloom tomatoes, thinly sliced
2 Vidalia onions, thinly sliced
1 teaspoon salt
½ teaspoon pepper
2 tablespoons basil, chopped
1 tablespoon oregano, chopped
½ cup aged cheddar cheese, shredded
½ cup mozzarella cheese, shredded
¼ cup Parmesan cheese, grated, plus more for sprinkling
2 tablespoons olive oil, plus more for drizzling

Roll pie crust to fit a 10-inch deep pie plate. Place crust into plate and refrigerate for 30 minutes.

Preheat oven to 375 degrees.

Remove pie crust from refrigerator and cover lightly with aluminum foil. Place dried beans on top of the foil and bake for 12 minutes. Remove foil and beans and return crust back into the oven for another 4-5 minutes or until crust is golden in color. Remove and place on cooling rack. Lightly brush mayonnaise on surface of crust and let cool completely.

Sprinkle ¼ of bread crumbs over bottom of crust. Layer half of the tomatoes, onions, salt, pepper, basil, oregano, cheddar cheese, mozzarella cheese, and Parmesan cheese. Repeat with another ¼ of breadcrumbs and remaining tomatoes, onions, salt, pepper, basil, oregano, and cheeses.

In a small bowl, combine olive oil and remaining breadcrumbs. Sprinkle breadcrumbs on top of tomato pie and finish with another drizzle of olive oil.

Bake the pie for about 1 hour or until hot and bubbly. Remove pie from oven and sprinkle with Parmesan cheese. Let pie cool for an hour and serve.

Tomato Soup

I remember as a child thinking, "who would eat tomato soup?" My only memory is my mother opening a can and enjoying this red soup. If I had been introduced to fresh ripe tomato soup I think this memory would be much different. I have to say, I dream of eating this scrumptious soup from the time I plant the tomatoes in the ground. There is just nothing like that first taste of summer in a bowl.

Tomatoes are considered one of the most heart-healthy foods. Fresh tomatoes help lower cholesterol and triglycerides. They are also a great source of lycopene, which is known for it's incredible antioxidant properties and aid in bone health.

Ingredients

3 pounds tomatoes
2 tablespoons butter
1 onion, chopped
2 carrots. chopped
1 cup vegetable stock
½ teaspoon basil, chopped
½ teaspoon oregano, chopped
Salt and pepper to taste

Preheat oven to 450 degrees. Stem and half tomatoes lengthwise, and then place tomatoes cut-side down on a lined cookie sheet and roast for 10 minutes. When tomatoes are cool enough to handle, remove skin and set aside.

Melt butter in heavy-bottomed stockpot. Add onion and carrots. Cook until soft.

Stir in tomatoes, stock, basil, and oregano. Bring to a boil, and then lower the heat to simmer. Cover pot and keep at simmer for about 20 minutes.

Carefully transfer mixture to a food processor and puree. Salt and pepper to taste.

Serving Suggestions: Warm tomato soup in a saucepan. Stir ⅓ cup of heavy cream into soup and bring to boil. Serve with salty crackers.

Basic Tomato Sauce

Basic Tomato Sauce Ingredients

5 tablespoons olive oil
1 large onion, diced
1 clove garlic, finely chopped
1 lb. tomatoes, fresh or canned, peeled,
And chopped with their juices
1 teaspoon salt
½ teaspoon pepper
3 basil leaves, chopped

Heat the oil in medium sauce pan. Add onions and cook over low to medium heat until translucent. Approximately 6 minutes.

Stir in garlic, tomatoes, salt, pepper, and basil. Cook for 30 minutes.

With immersion blender or food processor puree tomato mixture.

Adjust seasonings. Serve.

Homemade Pie Crust

Yields 2 10-inch pie crusts

Ingredients

3 cups all- purpose flour
1 teaspoon kosher salt
¾ cups unsalted butter (1 ½ sticks), very cold
⅓ cup vegetable shortening (Crisco), very cold
6 tablespoons ice water, plus more if dough is too thick.

Place flour and salt into food processor fitted with a steel blade and pulse to mix.

Dice butter. Add diced butter and cold shortening to processor. Add ice water to the mixture down the feed tube with machine running. Pulse machine until dough forms a ball. Wrap in plastic wrap. Refrigerate 30 minutes.

Cut dough in half. Roll one of the pieces on a well-floured board rolling from the center to the edge, turning and flouring the dough to make sure it does not stick.

Continue rolling until 14 inches in diameter. Fold the dough in half over the rolling pin, place in pie pan. Unfold and mold to pie plate.

If making a double crusted pie, roll remaining half of dough out on a well floured surface. Roll from the center to the edge, turning, flouring, and rolling until you get a disc with the diameter of approximately 12 inches or to desired size. Using a sharp knife, trim the edges of the top crust leaving a ¾ inch overhang under the original pie crust and crimp the edges using your index finger and thumb. Make steam vents by using a sharp knife to cut 4 slits in center of top crust.

If making a lattice crust, roll remaining half of dough into a rectangle about ⅛ inch thick and 8x10 inches. Cut the rectangle lengthwise into 1-inch strips. Make sure to do this on a floured surface so lattice strips do not stick. Place strips about one inch apart oven top of pie. Fold back every other strip half way over itself and place one of the remaining strips perpendicular to the original. Return the strips that had been folded back to their original position. Fold back the alternate strips and place another strip across the unfolded strips. Return strips that are folded back to the original position and repeat by continuing to weave the lattice on top of the pie filling. Roll the overhang under bottom pie crust. Use a sharp knife to trim off the excess. Use your index finger and thumb to pinch dough to make a fluted design.

Roasted Heirloom Cherry Tomatoes

Serves 4

Cherry tomatoes are the perfect side dish for any meal, breakfast, brunch, lunch, or dinner. I have friends that eat them like candy straight from the plant as snacks. Cherry tomatoes range from bright yellow and red to orange and pink and come in a variety of shapes and sizes. The color and shape alone add texture and eye appeal to any main course.

Ingredients

2 cups heirloom cherry tomatoes
¼ olive oil
2 tablespoons balsamic vinegar
1 tablespoon basil plus extra for garnish, chopped
1 tablespoon oregano plus extra for garnish, chopped
1 teaspoon salt
½ teaspoon pepper
½ cup Parmesan cheese (optional)

Preheat oven to 400 degrees.

In a medium bowl, mix together tomatoes, olive oil, balsamic vinegar, basil, oregano, salt, and pepper.

Pour tomatoes into a lined cookie sheet and place in oven for 10–12 minutes or until tomatoes caramelize.

Place tomatoes on a serving dish and garnish with basil and oregano. Sprinkle with Parmesan cheese. Serve warm.

Fresh cherry tomatoes will work in this recipe, but heirloom varieties taste much sweeter.

Vegetables and fruits of all shades contain phytonutrients including carotenoids and anthocyanin that produce the color in foods and help to protect your body. Choose colorful vegetables and fruits and stay healthy!

Tomato Vinaigrette

Ingredients

2 tablespoons salad vinegar
1 teaspoon sugar
½ shallot, minced
1 clove garlic, minced
½ teaspoon Kosher salt
¼ teaspoon pepper
1 ripe tomato
¼ cup olive oil

Place all ingredients in a food processor and as you pour oil in a stream slowly blend continually until emulsified.

Roasted Garden Vegetables

Serves 6

When I can no longer see my kitchen island for all the vegetables covering it, I know that it is time for Roasted Garden Vegetables. These vegetables pair well with any meat and are great on salads.

Ingredients

2 eggplants, cut in one inch cubes
2 tomatoes, quartered
2 red onions, quartered
1 red bell pepper, cut into 1 inch slices
1 yellow bell pepper, cut into 1-inch slices
Olive oil, for drizzling
2 tablespoons oregano
2 tablespoons basil
1 tablespoon kosher salt
1 tablespoon freshly ground pepper

Preheat oven to 450 degrees.

Place vegetables in groups on sheet pan. Do not crowd the pan or the vegetables will steam.

Sprinkle basil, salt and pepper over vegetables and roast for 15 minutes. Turn each piece and roast for 5 to 10 minutes more. Sprinkle with extra salt if needed and serve.

Jalapeño Poppers are one of my family's favorite summer snacks. There is just not much better than a cream and bacon filled fresh jalapeño with a crunchy crust!

Every year I inevitably plant more jalapeño plants than I really need – jalapeños happen to be my favorite – therefore, I am always looking for new ways to use them. Although I use them in chillies, soups, fajitas, and frittatas, my all-time favorite way to prepare jalapeños is as a Popper. I wish I had a plate of them now!

One of the reasons that I plant so many jalapeño peppers is for their health giving properties. They reduce cholesterol aggregation, help the heart to adjust to blood pressure changes, relieve congestion and migraine related pain, prevents certain cancers and even helps you to lose weight because of its thermogenic properties. I like to dry a portion of my peppers to have them all year round, but I love them most straight off the plant in their freshest form.

After testing many, many poppers in my quest for the best recipe, I have created one that exceeds them all. The bacon and sharp cheddar cheese in the filling add just the right amount of saltiness to balance the heat and acid of the jalapeño. The creamy filling is offset with the crunchy Panko coating giving the perfect balance of crunchy to creamy ratio. I really can't think of a better combination. It is a real keeper and I am privileged to share it with you.

Jalapeño Poppers

18 to 20 large jalapeños
8 ounces cream cheese, at room temperature
½ cup grated sharp cheddar cheese
8 strips bacon, cooked and crumbled
¾ cup all purpose flour
2 teaspoons Kosher salt, more for sprinkling
½ teaspoon cayenne
1 teaspoon garlic powder
2 large eggs, lightly beaten
¼ cup buttermilk
1 ½ cups Panko breadcrumbs
4 Tablespoons unsalted butter, melted

Preheat the oven to 350 degrees F.

Cut the jalapeño lengthwise creating a pocket for the filling. Leave the stem intact. Carefully scrape the inside of the jalapeño with a paring knife to remove the seeds.

In a small bowl, combine the cream cheese, cheddar cheese, and the bacon. Place the mixture in a resealable storage bag an cut one corner of the bag that will allow the mixture to be easily piped into the peppers. Squeeze the mixture to the bottom of the bag and fill each pepper with the cream cheese mixture. Press the edges of the pepper back together.

In a medium bowl, combine the flour, cayenne, garlic powder, eggs, and buttermilk and mix until the mixture looks like the consistency of pancake batter. It needs to be thick, but if you find that it is too thick, add a little more buttermilk. Place the Panko crumbs on a third dish. One at a time, coat the jalapeño in the batter, then press the jalapeño into the Panko crumbs gently to assure that the Panko adheres the jalapeño.

Place each pepper cut side up on a cookie sheet and spoon butter on top of each pepper. Bake for about 30 minutes or until the top is golden. Remove from the oven and transfer jalapeños to a serving dish and sprinkle with a little extra salt.

Corn

Corn, That's Maize to My Southern Ancestors

Throughout my entire life I have heard stories from my Granny's perspective of my appetite being only desirous of corn products when feasting at her home. She told of the dissension between herself and my parents over this issue. With such a wide array of healthy food, my choice was only limited to sweet corn and she understood this perfectly. She and I could not understand why my parent's were not on board with this!

Sweet corn. What could be better? Over 70% of American processed food contains some form of genetically modified ingredients mostly consisting of corn. That can be quite disturbing considering that the domesticated varieties used by the corporate farmers selling to the manufacturers contain Genetically Modified Organisms. These domesticated varieties cannot survive without the aid of humans. How bazar? Thankfully we can plant heirloom varieties. My favorite is Country Gentleman, a shoe peg variety of corn. It is a fine specimen. It needs to be cooked at once after picking it in that it begins losing its sugar content only a few minutes after it is picked from the stalk.

If you desire to save the seeds for next year's planting, beware of any neighboring farms growing hybrid corn. If the neighboring corn field is within a 1 to 2 mile radius, it will cross pollinate and your corn may then be subject to Genetically Modified Organisms.

Plant a flint variety of corn for grinding corn meal.

Corn Chowder

Serves 10–12

Corn chowder always reminds me of one my husband's best friends. He raves about my recipe and I think the secret to its success is the use of fresh corn. Although frozen corn is certainly acceptable, the fresh corn pops in your mouth and adds a special sweetness that is exceptional. I personally think the white cheddar cheese in the recipe gives this dish it's wow-factor, but this friend, whose name I can't disclose, is "allergic" to cheese. That's code for "I hate cheese"; therefore I make that optional in the recipe.

8 strips bacon, diced
2 large onions, chopped
⅓ cup flour
8 cups chicken stock
8 cups chopped potatoes
1 teaspoon salt
½ teaspoon pepper
8 ears fresh or 4 cups frozen corn
2 cups light cream (half and half)
1 tomato, diced
8 ounces sharp white cheddar cheese, optional

Sauté bacon and onion in heavy bottom stock pot. Drain excess fat.

Sprinkle flour on top of onion bacon mixture. Pour chicken stock, potatoes, salt, and pepper into pot and bring to a boil. Reduce to simmer for 15–20 minutes or until potatoes are tender.

Meanwhile, boil corn for 3–5 minutes. Drain and cut corn off the cob.

Add corn and cream into pot and heat through. Ladle into bowl and serve with tomatoes and, if desired, cheese.

Creamy Corn Pudding

Serves 4

This corn pudding is one of my all-time favorites for Christmas meals or alongside a BIG barbecue sandwich. It's one of the most versatile dishes I know. As a 5-year old, this was the only dish I would eat when I went to my grandmother's house. This, however, caused a lot of tension. My parents wanted me to eat a variety of foods and my granny wanted me to have "whatever the darling wants!"

Ingredients

4 tablespoons melted butter, divided
¼ cup bell peppers, diced
¼ cup onions, diced
2 tablespoons flour
½ teaspoon salt
¼ cup sugar
2 cups corn (fresh or frozen) Note: If using fresh corn, boil corn (on cob) for 3 minutes before cutting off the kernels. Try to scrape all the milk from the corn as you work.
1⅓ cup milk (for extra creamier pudding, replace the milk with half and half.)

Preheat oven to 325 degrees.

In a large sauté pan, sauté bell peppers and onions in 2 tablespoons of butter.

In a large bowl, mix flour, salt, sugar, and corn.

Add eggs, milk, remaining butter, and sautéed vegetables. Pour mixture into casserole. Place in a roasting pan and pour water halfway up the casserole.

Bake at 45 minutes or until pudding is golden brown.

You can use canned creamed corn as a substitute for the fresh or frozen corn.

To remove silk from corn use a wet paper towel.

When buying corn from the market, pick the ears with husks bright green, and the kernels full and milky.

Jalapeño Cornbread

Serves 6

This cornbread is great with just about anything, but especially soups, chili, and the like. The corn kernels give the cornbread extra texture that complements any dish.

If you are having a large crowd, you can double the recipe. You may have to leave it in the oven a little longer than the recipe calls for. To check for doneness, stick a toothpick into the center of the cornbread. If it comes out clean and the top is golden brown, it is ready.

Ingredients

¼ cup bacon drippings
(or the same amount of a vegetable oil)
½ cup buttermilk
½ cup sour cream
2 large eggs, beaten
½ cup corn, fresh or frozen
1 jalapeño chile, minced and seeded
1 cup cornmeal
1½ teaspoons baking powder
½ teaspoon baking soda
½ teaspoon salt

Preheat oven to 400 degrees.

Heat drippings in 9" skillet until sizzling hot.

Meanwhile, combine sour cream, buttermilk, eggs, corn, and chile in large bowl. Stir in cornmeal, baking powder, baking soda, and salt.

Pour dripping from skillet into cornbread mixture and mix well. The drippings should sizzle when it hits the batter. Pour batter into skillet.

Bake for 30 minutes or until golden brown.

Heirloom Gardening Tips

1. Always order seeds from a reputable source such as Rareseeds.com or Southernexposure.com.

2. Be sure to get your soil tested in the winter to adjust the ph. Send your soil to your local extension office for results. This tip will save money and headaches.

3. Many seeds need a head start indoors. Try not to be too hasty to plant because if plants are left indoors too long, they will become weak and lanky. It is best to move them outdoors when the plants produce their second set of leaves.

4. Be careful to acclimate the plants that have been indoors for a few days to a week on a porch or near the house in the shade before planting in the ground. This gives them a chance to get accustomed to the bright sun and temperature.

5. Keep a garden journal or layout of what you are planting and where you are planting so that the subsequent spring you can rotate your crops. This will improve soil structure and decrease the likelihood of pests.

6. When saving seeds, choose your most robust and favorite plants to extract the seeds. Always store them in a dry, cool, and dark location. I like to use 4 ounce glass mason jars and store them in the refrigerator. The seeds should last for years.

Roasted Okra

Serves 4 to 6

Okra is a "love it" or "hate it" kind of vegetable. I think it is all in the preparation just like most ingredients. People do not like it in that it can become very slimy, but if made correctly, you can have the flavor without the slime. In the South, it is a "must have" in soups and gumbo. In the preparation for this recipe, the okra has a little heat and is slightly crunchy on the outside. Make sure you pick your okra or choose okra from the farmer's market or store that is no more than 3 inches long. The smaller the okra, the more tender the bite.

Ingredients

1 pound young okra (less than 3 inches)
¼ cup olive oil
1½ tablespoons cumin
1½ teaspoon salt
1 teaspoon black pepper
½ teaspoon chipotle chili pepper

Preheat oven to 400 degrees.

Toss okra in olive oil to coat. Combine all dry spices and toss with okra.

Place okra onto a sheet pan in a single layer.

Bake for 5-7 minutes and turn okra over onto the other side. Bake for another 3-5 minutes or until pods are softened.

Eggplant Lasagna

Serves 10

This is an extremely healthful, low fat, full of flavor meal. The robust flavors of the tomato sauce and pesto paired with the saltiness of the ricotta would satisfy the healthiest of appetites.

Ingredients

3 tablespoons olive oil, plus more for sautéing
1 tablespoon fresh oregano, chopped
1 teaspoon salt fresh thyme, chopped
½ teaspoons Kosher salt
½ teaspoon freshly ground pepper
3 medium eggplant
2 cups tomato sauce
2 cups ricotta cheese
1 cup pesto (page 113)
2 cups mozzarella cheese, shredded
Fresh basil, for garnish

Preheat oven to 350 degrees.

Slice eggplant into ⅛ inch slices using a very sharp knife or mandolin.

In a large bowl mix olive oil, oregano, thyme, salt, and pepper. Toss eggplant in mixture.

Heat a nonstick sauté pan over high heat. When oil is simmering place eggplant and sauté until pliable.

Spoon about ½ cup tomato sauce on bottom of 9x11 baking dish. Place a layer of eggplant then more tomato sauce. Dollop ricotta and pesto using about ⅓ of each ingredient. Add another layer of eggplant slices and repeat twice more with the tomato, ricotta, and pesto. Top with mozzarella cheese.

Bake for 35 to 40 minutes or until cheese is bubbly and lightly browned. Garnish with fresh basil leaves.

Cantaloupe grew profusely in our garden this year so we decided to try a few "experimental" recipes. This recipe ended up being a real "keeper." Scott said it was his favorite ice cream EVER! Now that is something to remember.

Side note: Cantaloupe is known to help those who have insomnia by reducing the bodies heart rate, reduces stress, and helps to you relax.

Cantaloupe Ice Cream

Yields about six cups

Ingredients

2 cups peeled and cubed cantaloupe
5/6 cup granulated sugar divided
(1/3 cup and 1/2 cup)
1 1/2 tablespoons fresh lime juice
1 3/4 cups half and half
1 1/4 cup coconut milk

Preparation:

In a large bowl, combine the cubed cantaloupe with 1/3 cup of sugar. Cover and marinate at least 6 hours in the refrigerator.

In a saucepan over medium-low heat, simmer the marinated cantaloupe pieces in the juices of the marinade. Cook for 5 minutes, stirring occasionally, then remove and cool.

Puree the cantaloupe mixture in a blender or food processor. Add the lime juice and process again. Cover and chill for an hour.

In a large bowl, combine the half and half and coconut milk with the remaining 1/2 cup of sugar. Stir in the pureed cantaloupe, stirring gently to mix in.

Place mixture in the freezer for about 2 hours. Transfer to an ice cream maker and proceed with the manufacturer's instructions for making ice cream.

Place the cantaloupe ice cream into an air tight container and return to freezer for 2 hours before serving.

CANDIED MAPLE WALNUTS

Yields 1 Cup

Want a perfect topping? The combination of walnuts, maple syrup, and salt is your answer. I usually make a double batch because they are so good. I eat them before they make it to their intended destination.

4 ounces (1 cup) walnuts, chopped
1/4 cup maple syrup
Pinch of salt

Sauté walnuts in maple syrup for about 3 to 5 minutes or until the syrup begins to turn color and the nuts are toasted. Watch closely as you sauté because caramelizing is one step away from burning.

Remove walnuts from heat and place on a sheet of wax paper and let cool completely.

Use immediately or store in a airtight container for up to 2 weeks.

Poached Pears

Serves 6

I once was told that poached pears were a favorite in Italy. No matter... I know they are a favorite around here. I love to make these beauties for breakfast as well as serve them as a lovely dessert.

Different pears will cook at different rates depending on size, type, and ripeness. You will know they are done when a knife pierces easily into the pear.

To keep pears from discoloring, they must be basted frequently. It helps to have the pears fit snugly together.

Ingredients

Butter, for greasing casserole
6 ripe pears
1 cup orange juice
1 cup water
¼ cup of honey
½ teaspoon vanilla extract
⅛ teaspoon ground cinnamon
Zest of 1 orange

Preheat oven to 375 degrees. Butter a casserole just large enough to hold the pears.

Peel pears leaving stems. Slice bottom of pears flat so it stands upright. With a melon baller, scoop out the inside of pears through the bottom and remove seeds. Stand pears upright in casserole.

Add orange juice and water to the casserole and bake the pears for about 40 minutes or until you can pierce with a fork easily. Baste.

Transfer pears to a plate. Leave the oven on. Pour juices into a bowl and add honey, cinnamon, vanilla, and orange zest. Mix well. Place pears back into casserole and drizzle honey mixture over pears. You may not need all the mixture. Place pears back into the oven for 5 more minutes.

Stand a pear in a bowl. Garnish with mint leaves. Serve with the honey mixture and your favorite chocolate sauce and whipped cream.

Panko is made by baking bread via electrical current. It creates a bread without a crust and is then ground into fine crumbs. They give extra crunch, but the regular bread crumbles will do just fine for this recipe.

Between slicing each slice of goat cheese wipe your knife with a warm wet towel. If your slices crumble just use your finger to mold it back together.

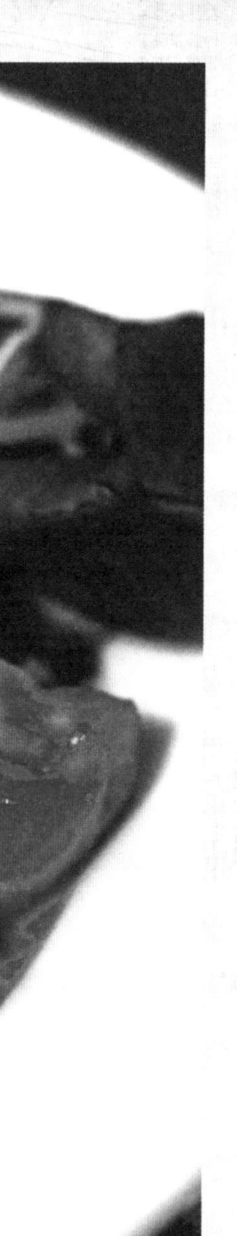

Spinach, Arugula, and Crispy Fried Goat Cheese Salad with Tomato Vinaigrette

In our family we have a tradition of taking one of our children out every week. On one of these nights we went to a farm to table restaurant where we had this absolutely awesome salad packed full of flavor. I wanted to replicate the salad and I think I have gotten pretty close.

Ingredients

2 cups spinach leaves
2 cups arugula
½ cup tomatoes, roughly chopped
16 oz. goat cheese
2 eggs, beaten
1 cup Panko
2 teaspoons diced parsley
1 teaspoon diced thyme
1 pinch salt
½ teaspoon freshly ground black pepper
½ cup flour
olive oil for frying
Tomato Vinaigrette (page 44)

Place goat cheese log in freezer for 15 minutes to make it easier to slice.

Place flour into a shallow dish or plate. In a second shallow dish, beat eggs. In a third dish, stir panko, parsley, thyme, salt, and pepper until combined.

Remove cheese from freezer and slice into ½ inch rounds.

Coat cheese in flour, then egg mixture, then Panko mixture. Repeat with remaining cheese and set aside.

In a non-stick sauté pan, place just enough oil to cover the bottom. Heat oil on high heat. Once oil is simmering, place coated cheese in pan for about 1 to 2 minutes. Do not crowd the pan or it will steam instead of fry. Turn cheese over and cook for another minute or until cheese is golden. Remove cheese from pan and transfer to a paper towel. Repeat with remaining cheese.

Meanwhile, in a large bowl, mix spinach, arugula and tomatoes. Spoon 4 tablespoons of Tomato Vinaigrette and toss gently.

Divide salad mix onto 4 plates. Divide fried cheese among the plates and drizzle extra tomato vinaigrette as desired. Serve immediately.

Spiced Pumpkin Butter

Before I began growing heirloom pumpkins, I had absolutely no desire to eat pumpkin butter, pumpkin pie, or any other kind of pumpkin treat—and that's saying something, since I can be tempted to eat just about any dessert. My husband Scott, on the other hand, loves pumpkin and will even choose pumpkin pie over chocolate at Thanksgiving! I find that very hard to understand.

Our first year of gardening together, Scott insisted on experimenting with every kind of pumpkin that he thought would grow in our area. We had pumpkins busting out of our ears! To my amazement, pumpkin became my favorite vegetable that year. The first recipe I tried was a sensational pumpkin soup, which convinced me to do a little research to figure out what makes fresh pumpkin taste so different from canned.

Pumpkin, brown sugar, cider, and spices—what's not to love?

I discovered something surprising: The canned "pumpkin" you find in the grocery store is actually made from butternut squash. It seems the word "pumpkin" generally refers to the broader category of winter squash. Aha.

So when Scott asked me to make pumpkin butter, I harvested several of the small pumpkins from our patch to make the puree. What a difference from store-bought! This puree was sweeter, had less moisture, and tasted both different and better than the canned version I was used to. And the pumpkin butter? It's now one of my very favorite things to eat.

Find out for yourself how different and delicious fresh pumpkin tastes by trying my Spiced Pumpkin Butter recipe for yourself.

READY-MADE PIE FILLING

Simply mix 2 cups of pumpkin butter in a large bowl with 2 eggs
1 yolk from a third egg
1½ cups heavy cream
½ teaspoon lemon zest

Place the mixture into an unbaked pie shell, then bake at 350 degrees for 40 to 50 minutes.

SPICED PUMPKIN BUTTER

Ingredients

4½ pounds (about 7 cups) pumpkin puree
(preferably from small- to medium-sized sugar pumpkins)
1 pound brown sugar
1 cinnamon stick broken into pieces
½ whole nutmeg
6 cloves allspice
¾ cup apple cider

Cut each pumpkin in half and scrape out the seeds (save and toast them for a treat), then discard any stringy parts. Place pumpkins flesh-side down on a cookie sheet lined with a silpat or foil. Bake pumpkins at 350 degrees for about an hour or until fork-tender. Remove pumpkins from the oven, let them cool, then scoop out the pulp and place it into a medium-sized saucepan.

Using a mortar and pestle or a clean coffee mill, grind the spices to a fine powder. Stir sugar, spices, and apple cider into the saucepan with the pumpkin.

Simmer the mixture over low heat for 1 to 1½ hours. It will thicken as you continue to cook, eventually reaching the consistency of butter. While thickening, it may stick to the bottom of the pan. No worries! You will know the pumpkin butter is ready when a wooden spoon leaves a clear path across the bottom of the pan.

Ladle into jars, seal, and store in the fridge for up to 3 weeks. Or, let the butter cool, then ladle into freezer bags or freezer-safe mason jars (leave plenty of head space) and store in the freezer for up to six months.

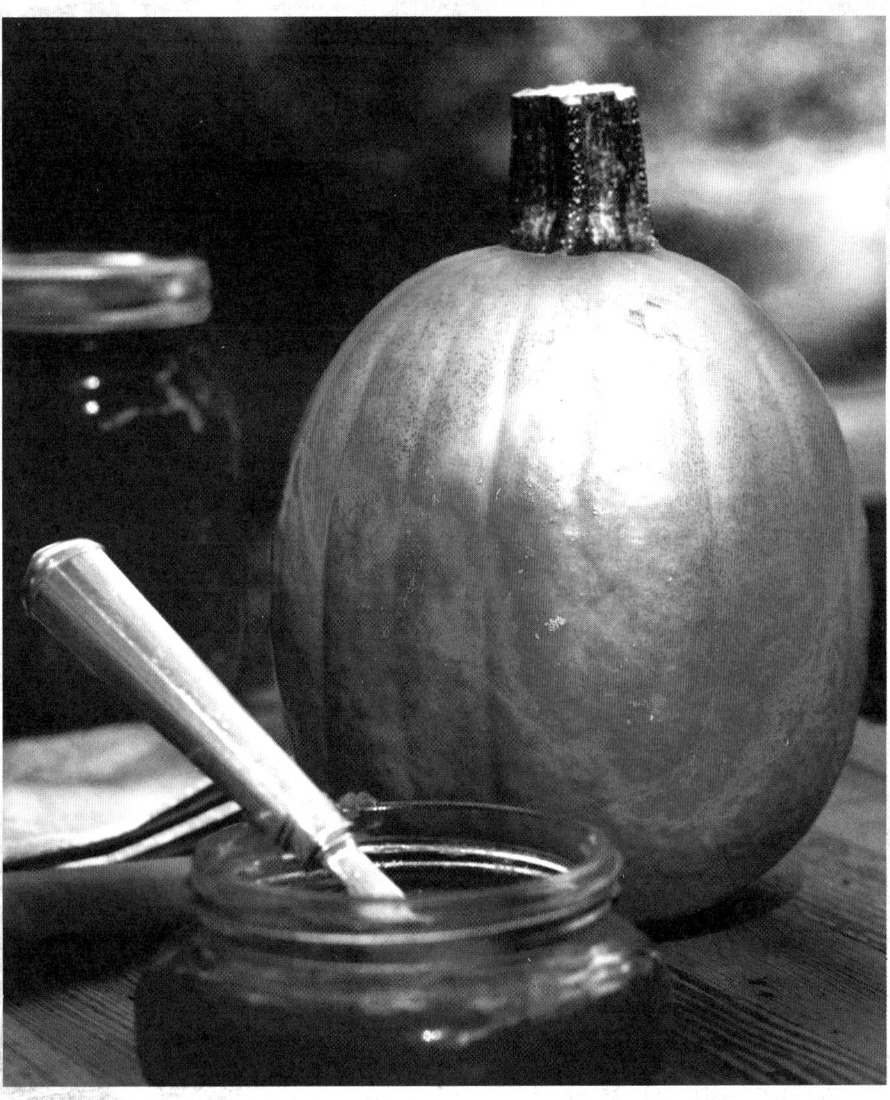

I have always had pumpkin out of the can until I started growing my own. Pumpkin actually has a fantastic flavor on its own with very little need to enhance the flavor. This experiment with pumpkin pie "pioneer style" was quite exceptional.

It was one of those nights that will go down in my memory bank as a nostalgic moment. Everything seemed to be so perfect.

When the settlers came to their new nation they obviously were living off the land. They had to learn from the Indians and enjoy the foods that the natives enjoyed. They had no electricity and cooked quite differently than we do in this modern age. I thought that it would be great fun to cook pumpkins straight on the smoldering coals of a once nice fire just as the settlers did.

HOW TO MAKE PUMPKIN PIE "PIONEER STYLE"

You will need to start your fire about an hour before you want to start cooking the pumpkins so that you will be placing them on hot coals as opposed to a blazing fire.

To prepare the pumpkin, the kids and I removed the tops of 4 medium-sized pumpkin and scraped the seeds and stringy insides out of the pumpkin's cavity. In a small bowl, I mixed 4 cups of heavy cream, ½ teaspoon freshly ground cinnamon, ¼ teaspoon freshly ground ginger, 1 cup of sugar, and ¼ teaspoon of salt. I poured one cup of the mixture into each pumpkin and took them outside and put them on the hot coals.

The pumpkins were not done all at the same time. Some of my coals happened to be hotter in spots and my pumpkins varied in size. On average, it took about an hour for the pumpkins to bake to completion. I carefully removed the pumpkins from the fire and placed them in a small cast iron skillet. Be very careful here not to puncture the skin because the mixture will begin to leak from punctured areas.

Mix the tender pumpkin with the cream mixture. You can eat this straight from the pumpkin or remove it to a large bowl and puree it even further for a smoother texture and use it for a base for pie filling.

I served our "pumpkin pie" straight from pudding bowls. My family loved it.

Please note that when it is not puréed, it has a texture that resembles a soft spaghetti squash. My family are used to eating my "experiments," but if you are used to eating the canned pumpkin or the puréed pumpkin, this may not be your favorite.

TO MAKE A MORE TRADITIONAL PIE

Simply mix 2 cups of the pumpkin purée in a large bowl with 2 eggs, 1 yolk from a third egg, and ½ teaspoon lemon zest. Place the mixture into an unbaked pie shell, then bake at 350 degrees for 40 to 50 minutes.

All in all, this night was one to be remembered and I will "bake" my pumpkins from now on right over hot coals. The time is well spent with family as we talked, ate our outdoor dinner, and waited for our pumpkin desserts. I hope this gives you an idea for your family and that you enjoy them and the outdoors as much as I did that wonderful simple night.

Broccoli has always been one of the greatest side dish ingredients of all time. Most kids don't like it very much, but I happened to be one kid who LOVED it. My mom served it to me, cooked in various ways, at least three times a week growing up.

Now that I have my own family, I still eat a lot of broccoli. It's not just about the taste, either — broccoli is packed full of vitamins and minerals, low in calories, and high in fiber, plus it contains multiple nutrients with potent anti-cancer properties. (Just don't boil it — that saps a lot of the nutrition.)

Roasting broccoli, which is my favorite way to prepare it, both seals in the vitamins and minerals and brings out the complex flavor of this wonder vegetable. One of the great things about roasting is that you can change the flavor profile of a vegetable simply by using different seasonings and spices. Roasting makes it super easy to match broccoli to any kind of cuisine, including Asian, Italian, and Mediterranean.

The trick to making an awesome broccoli dish is to use the freshest bunch you can get. If you grow your own broccoli, like I do, be sure to harvest it in the early morning, before the soil heats up. This will ensure a sweeter, less bitter taste in the final dish. (Harvested more than you can use in growing season? Blanch the extra for about 3 minutes, place it into freezer bags, and freeze for up to a year.)

Roasted Broccoli with Toasted Bread Crumbs and Pine Nuts is one of my family's all-time favorite broccoli recipes. The toasted bread crumbs and pine nuts give this dish both a special crunch and an earthiness that everyone seems to enjoy. I hope that you like it as much as we do!

Roasted Broccoli with Toasted Bread Crumbs and Pine Nuts

Serves 6 to 8

Ingredients

2 pounds broccoli, rinsed and trimmed
4 cloves garlic, thinly sliced
1 teaspoon Kosher salt
¼ teaspoon freshly ground pepper
2 to 3 pinches red pepper flakes
¾ cup olive oil
½ finely grated Parmesan cheese
½ cup toasted pine nuts (optional)
Splash good balsamic vinegar

Preheat oven to 425 degrees.

Cut the broccoli florets into bite-sized pieces and the stalks into very thin (⅛-inch) rounds. In a medium-sized mixing bowl, combine broccoli, garlic, salt, pepper, red pepper flakes, bread crumbs, and olive oil; mix well.

Spread broccoli mixture onto a cookie sheet and place in the oven for 8 to 10 minutes. Meanwhile, heat a sauté pan to medium heat and toast pine nuts about 3 minutes.

Remove broccoli from the oven, toss in the cheese and pine nuts, and place mixture in a serving dish. Drizzle balsamic vinegar over the broccoli and serve immediately.

Garlic Mashed Potatoes

Serves 8

Mashed potatoes are the ultimate comfort food that accompanies just about any dish. The added garlic gives these perfect-mashed potatoes that extra punch that brings an ordinary meal up a notch.

Hint: To avoid gummy potatoes, only add warm ingredients to the potatoes (warm butter and cream) and drain potatoes completely removing as much water as possible.

Ingredients

4 pounds Idaho potatoes, peeled and cut into 1 inch pieces
½ cup butter, melted
1 cup half and half, warmed
1 cup heavy cream, warmed
6 garlic cloves, finely minced
Salt
Freshly ground black pepper

Place potatoes in a large Dutch oven. Cover potatoes with salted water and bring to a boil. Reduce heat to medium and cook potatoes until tender, about 15 minutes. Remove from heat and drain. Return potatoes to pot and place back on stove.

With a potato masher, slowly integrate the butter and half and half. Add the heavy cream and garlic and mix in with an electric mixer on medium speed until smooth. If potatoes are too stiff add more cream. Add salt and pepper to taste.

Potatoes grow from pieces of potatoes or whole potatoes planted in rich soil. The tubers will grow underground. Once the plant blooms and you see it flower, the potatoes are ready to harvest.

Sweet Potatoes

Sweet Potatoes, Everything's Sweeter in the South

The first year my family attempted to grow sweet potatoes, we waited and waited for the leaves to arrive on the plant. Everyday we checked the plants and the stems seemed to be at a stand still with no leaves. The poor grass like stems looked as if they had been freshly mowed with a lawn mower. I could not sleep one night and began looking out the window at 3 am, and I finally had the answer to the "root" of the problem; a doe and three fawns! We learned quickly to protect these obviously luscious plants from the hungry deer.

Sweet potatoes will last for up to 6 months if cured and stored properly. The natural sweetness of sweet potatoes improves with proper curing. Store sweet potatoes at around 85 degrees for 10 days. I use my back porch in that Alabama remains hot during sweet potato's harvest season. After the curing process, move the sweet potatoes to a storage place such as a basement or root cellar kept between 55 and 60 degrees.

Sweet Potato "baked" Fries

Serves 4 to 6

Ingredients
2 pounds potatoes, cut into ½ inch strips (fries)
3 tablespoons olive oil
1 tablespoon cumin
½ teaspoon salt
¼ teaspoon cayenne pepper

Preheat oven to 425 degrees.

Bring a large stockpot of water to a boil. Place potatoes in pot and boil for about 6-8 minutes or until al dente.

Drain potatoes and then dry with paper towels.

Mix remaining ingredients in medium sized bowl. Place potatoes in the mixture and coat evenly.

Spread sweet potatoes on a cookie sheet. Use two cookie sheets if potatoes are touching or potatoes will steam instead of roast.

Place potatoes in oven for 30 minutes or until golden and crispy turning them occasionally.

Remove and serve with Chipotle Dipping Sauce.

Chipotle Dipping Sauce

If you want to cheat on the homemade mayonnaise, use Hellman's mayonnaise.

1 cup Homemade Mayonnaise (page 185)
1 ripe (red) jalapeño
½ lemon, juiced
Pinch of salt

Heat a cast iron skillet to smoking hot. Place jalapeño on skillet and cover with lid or pan to create roasting affect. Rotate pepper occasionally (once a minute), until all sides are charred. Remove stem and skin from pepper.

Place pepper along with the rest of the ingredients into a food processor and blend until smooth. Check seasoning and serve.

Cinnamon sugar sweet potato fries

Replace the dry ingredients with ¼ cup sugar, 1 tablespoon cinnamon, and ¼ teaspoon nutmeg and continue with recipe instructions.

I often eat these all-around winner fries as a meal. The savory fries are great piled up under venison or organic beef steak, and the sweeter version, Cinnamon Sugar Sweet Potato Fries, are perfect as a dessert. Surprisingly, both the savory and sweet fries are delicious with the Chipotle Dipping Sauce (page 80).

Side note: You may be tempted to skip boiling the potatoes, but this step helps the potatoes to be crispy on the outside and tender on the inside. It is well worth it!

Mashed Sweet Potatoes

Serves 6

You can't go wrong serving sweet potatoes with steak, quail, venison, and some fish dishes. Not only are they a healthy choice, they bring an earthy quality that gives a subtle comfort. The Southerner's garden would not be complete without this perfect root vegetable.

Nature's perfect beauty food? Sweet potatoes contain twice as much fiber as the other potatoes and is full of vitamin B6, A, C, and E. These nutrients contribute to a glowing complexion and vibrant healthy hair.

Ingredients

3 pounds sweet potatoes, peeled and cut into chunks
4 tablespoons (½ stick) butter
½ cup packed brown sugar
½ teaspoon nutmeg
Salt and pepper, to taste

Place potatoes in large pot and add water to just cover them. Set heat to high and boil potatoes until tender, and then drain.

Place potatoes back into the pot and fold in butter and sugar until dissolved. Blend in spices with a hand mixer until well incorporated and potatoes are smooth. Serve hot with extra butter!

Creamy Sweet Potato Soup

Serves 6 to 8

Ingredients

6 medium sweet potatoes (about 3½ lbs.)
1 pear, seeded and quartered
olive oil, for sautéing and frying
Kosher salt
pepper
1 Vidalia onion, chopped
3 celery ribs, chopped
2 cloves garlic, minced
1 red jalapeño pepper
18 basil leaves
¼ teaspoon ground nutmeg
¼ teaspoon ground ginger
4 to 6 cups vegetable stock
1 cup whipping cream
1 small log goat cheese

Preheat oven to 425 degrees. Roughly chop 5 of the sweet potatoes. Spread sweet potatoes and pear pieces onto a cookie sheet lined with parchment paper. Add a light coating of olive oil along with a sprinkling of salt and pepper, then place in the oven for about 25 minutes or until a fork easily pierces through the potato chunks.

Meanwhile, heat a skillet with a little olive oil until just hot. Add the onion and celery, and sauté for about 3 minutes or until the vegetables are translucent. Add the garlic and sauté a minute more. While these vegetables are cooking, slice the remaining sweet potato and the red jalapeño pepper as thinly as possible.

In another pan, add about ¼ inch of olive oil and fry the basil leaves; these will fry quickly, so keep an eye on them. Remove the leaves to a paper towel to drain, then repeat the process with the sweet potato and jalapeño strips. (It should take about 2 minutes to fry the sweet potato and less than a minute to fry the pepper.)

Remove roasted vegetables from the oven and place them into a food processor along with the nutmeg, ginger, vegetable stock, and whipping cream. Transfer the onions, celery, and garlic to the food processor and purée the ingredients until smooth. Adjust seasonings to desired taste.

Divide soup among 6 bowls and garnish each with 3 basil leaves, 3 or 4 sweet potato chips and a few fried jalapeño pepper strips. Crumble goat cheese over the soup and serve immediately.

Creamy Sweet Potato Soup is one of those soups I devour. The sweet and creamy texture with the tartness of the goat cheese and the crunch of the fried sweet potatoes and basil makes this my go-to recipe during sweet potato harvest season!

Sweet Potato Biscuits

Serves 8

Ingredients

2 cups all-purpose flour
1 tablespoon baking powder
¼ teaspoon baking soda
1 teaspoon Kosher salt
6 tablespoons unsalted butter, frozen
¾ cup buttermilk
1 cup baked, mashed sweet potato (about 1 medium to large potato)

Preheat oven to 400 degrees. Combine dry ingredients in a large bowl. In a separate bowl, mix milk and sweet potatoes until combined.

Cut frozen butter into small cubes and blend into the flour mixture using your fingers. Take care not to melt the butter (handle as little as possible). Add wet mixture into the dry and lightly mix dough with your hands to combine. Bring the mixture together and once together turn out onto a floured surface (the dough will look very shaggy). Press it into a 9 x 6 rectangle (approximately 2 inches thick). Cut the dough into rounds. Gather leftover dough, and repeat until you have 8 large biscuits. If you want a lot of small biscuits, roll dough out to ¾ inch thickness and cut biscuits using the size cutter you would like.

Place biscuits in a skillet and bake until bottoms turn golden brown, about 12 – 15 minutes.

Southern Collards

Serves 8

Collard greens are an all-time favorite in the South. They pair well with just about any protein or a well-balanced vegetable plate. My mom loves to eat a big bowl of these earthy greens with crumbled jalapeño cornbread for a very satisfying meal. If you ever try it this way, you will be hooked for life!

Collard greens are loaded with Vitamin K which helps with increasing bone mass and decreases the effects of Alzheimer's disease by limiting neuronal damage.

Soak the entire bunch of leaves in salt water for about 30 minutes then rinse the greens in running water for about 3 minutes before cooking fresh collards.

Ingredients

Olive oil
1 onion, chopped
1 tablespoon garlic
2 pounds collards, washed and pulled from the stem
2 cups wine
4 cups broth
14 teaspoon red pepper flakes
1 tablespoon kosher salt
¼ tablespoon freshly ground pepper

Heat olive oil in a large sauté pan over medium heat. Sweat the onions until they are translucent, about 5 minutes. Add garlic and continue to cook for 30 seconds longer.

Place washed collards into sauté pan. You may have to add half of the greens to the pan and let them shrink and then add the other half. Add wine, broth, red pepper flakes, salt, and pepper to the pan. Bring mixture to a boil and lower to simmer for 1 hour.

My daughters made these turnip root fries for Scott and I on our anniversary this year. They loaded them with cheese, bacon, chives, and luscious sour cream that made turnips addictive! Interestingly, many are born with a "sensitive" gene that makes turnips twice as bitter as those born with two "insensitive" genes.

These loaded turnip root fries are not only scrumptious, they are super healthy and great for those of you on a low carb diet!

Loaded Turnip Root Baked Fries

Serves 2 to 4

Ingredients

3-4 pound turnip roots, washed and peeled
3 tablespoons butter, melted
¼ cup vegetable oil, melted
1 tablespoon salt
½ teaspoon pepper
½ teaspoon smoked paprika
¼ teaspoon garlic powder
1 cup sharp cheddar cheese
½ cup Parmesan cheese
4 ounces sour cream
½ pound bacon, fried and crumbled
½ bunch green onions, finely chopped

Preheat oven to 425 degrees.

Cut turnip root into one to two (maybe 3 to 4) inch thick fries. In a medium saucepan, melt butter and vegetable oil. Place fries in the pan with the melted butter and oil and coat well. Add salt, pepper, smoked paprika, and garlic powder to the fries and incorporate until distributed evenly.

Pour the fries onto a baking sheet, and bake for about 25 to 35 minutes or until crisp on the outside, but tender on the inside. Plate the fries. Sprinkle cheeses over the fries then dollop with the sour cream. Sprinkle bacon and chives over the fries and dig in.

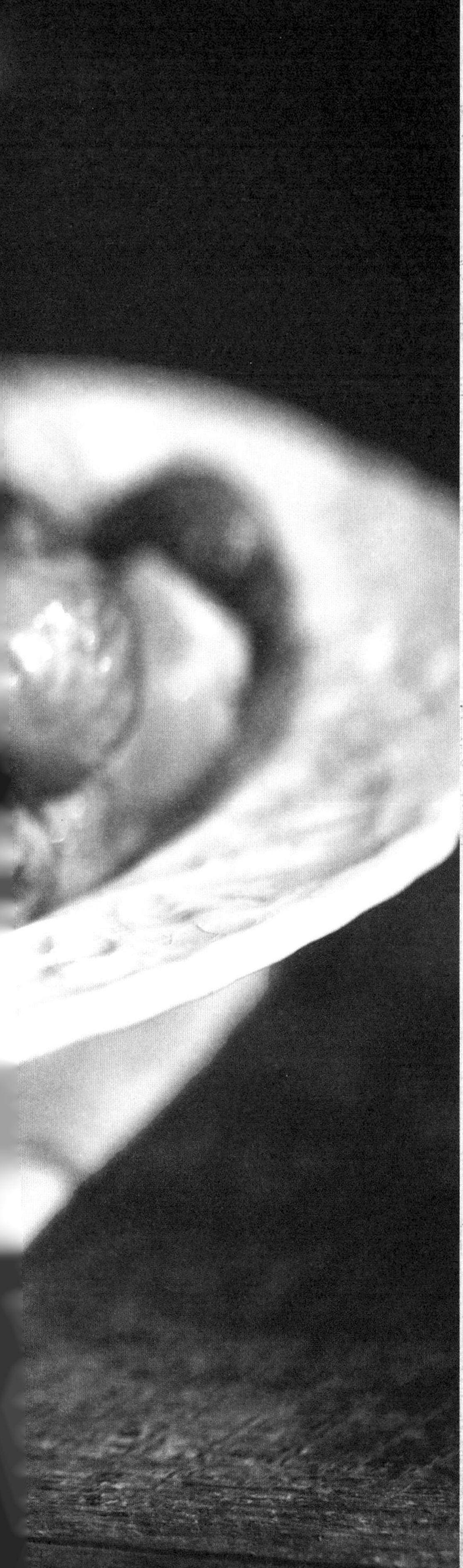

Creamed Brussels Sprouts

Serves 6

When I mention Brussels sprouts most everyone I know contorts their faces in such a way that demonstrates disgust until they try this recipe. People that have hated Brussels sprouts their entire lives admit them to now be one of their beloved vegetables. My kids eat them like candy!

Ingredients

1 quart Brussels sprouts
2 tablespoons butter, melted
¾ cup boiling whipping cream
Salt and pepper

Preheat oven to 350 degrees.

Trim stem and outer layer of the Brussels sprouts.

In a stock pot, blanch sprouts for 3 minutes in boiling water. Drain and place sprouts in a casserole arranged in a single layer.

Pour butter over sprouts and sprinkle with salt and pepper. Place in oven for 10 minutes.

Pour cream over sprouts and bake for 10 more minutes or until sprouts are tinder. Correct seasoning and serve as soon as possible.

Vertical and Container Gardening: Grow and Cook in Small Spaces

No Space, No Problem: Vertical and Container Gardening

There should be nothing that holds you back from gardening. Do you have limited space, time, your house is on a small lot, or live in an apartment? Vertical and container gardens are two fantastic ways to manage your favorite fruits, vegetables, and herbs in a small space and yield produce as if you had a large space. Container gardening is a perfect way to teach your little ones how to care for and nurture a garden as well as build confidence.

Vertical gardening has many advantages and is used in large gardens as well as small gardens. Not only does it save space, the plant becomes less prone to pests and disease because the plant is off the ground. Plants use less water when grown vertically as well as shade herbs and vegetables that need a little less sun. The best plants to grow vertically are cucumbers, green beans, and peas. I also like to plant vertically in containers by planting cherry tomatoes, surrounded by basil, oregano, thyme and other Italian herbs.

Trellis' can be built easily by using fallen limbs and tying them together in the shape of a tee pee or by simply using lattice board giving plants a place to climb. When building your vertical structure, make sure your structure can

support the weight of the vine and plants. One of my friends has a cucumber trellis growing on her porch to block an unsightly view. These trellis' can also be planted on porches to give you more privacy.

I love walking by my beautiful yet functional container gardens! Not only are they gorgeous, I get the same amount of produce as if using a square foot of garden space. Using containers is inexpensive and less time consuming in that you have the soil ready year after year with only having to amend the nutrients in the soil a little before each growing season. Bird baths, half of a wooden rain barrel, or old fountains make great unusual containers.

Even if you choose to plant only a few plants in a pot, you will be rewarded!

Refrigerator Dill Pickles

Yields 2 quarts

With as many babies as I have had, you know I know pickles! No really. These really are the greatest pickles and go great with Quarter Pound Turkey Burgers.

Ingredients

1½ pounds fresh pickling cucumbers
2 onions, thinly sliced
8 sprigs of dill
1 teaspoon whole allspice
3 cups water
1 cup distilled white vinegar
½ cup sugar
4 tablespoons salt
6 cloves garlic, smashed
1½ teaspoon dill seed

Slice cucumbers and onions into ¼ inch rounds. Divide the slices evenly among 2 quart-sized sterilized jars. Add 4 sprigs of dill and ½ teaspoon of whole allspice to each jar.

Combine water, vinegar, sugar, salt, garlic, and dill seed in a medium saucepan. Bring to a boil then lower to simmer and cook for 5 minutes.

Ladle hot liquid into jars, leaving 1-inch headspace. Set jars aside and let cool completely. Place lids securely on jars and store in refrigerator. They should last for up to 6 weeks.

To Soak *or* not *to* Soak

"Take your time" has never really been a phrase that my mind has really grasped very well. I pretty much attempt to do all things full speed ahead and attempt to find a way to use the least amount of time and energy to reach a desired purpose. Reluctantly, I must confess that I thought soaking beans, peas, and the likes was a huge waste of time and for years I just rinsed my beans before cooking them.

My flippant, rushed attitude about the soaking procedure was a huge mistake. I am learning that patience is always rewarded and that there is a reason for the "madness" of waiting. Without soaking your beans and peas, digestive ills such as gas, heartburn, and reflux are a likely result.

Upon soaking legumes in cold water, phytic acid and enzyme inhibitors are released producing a scum that rises to the top of the water. Once the scum is removed, you are much less vulnerable to bloating and digestive issues. Go now and enjoy your favorite 15 bean soup or a huge bowl of healthy black-eyed peas and homemade jalapeño cornbread!

Heirloom Black-eyed Peas

Serves 8

Eating black-eyed peas at my grandfather's house has always been a family tradition for bringing in the New Year. Growing up in the South, we have such an abundance of black-eyed peas, crowder peas, and butter beans from our gardens that we can and freeze them for an entire year's use. It is a staple in the Southern home and pairs well with fish and venison as well as being a main dish on its own accompanied with Jalapeño Cornbread.

Make sure the bell pepper does not overcook. It will lose its color and its al dente texture.

Ingredients

4 cups heirloom fresh black-eyed peas
4 cups water or chicken stock
1 tablespoon butter
1 tablespoon kosher salt
½ red bell pepper, diced
2 tablespoons olive oil
¼ Vidalia onion, diced

Place black-eyed peas, chicken stock, butter, and salt into large saucepan. Bring to a boil, and then lower to simmer.

Meanwhile sauté bell peppers in olive oil until al dente. When peas are done (about 30 minutes of simmering) pour into bowl and sprinkle bell peppers and raw onions on top. Serve.

Peas have an abundance of nitrogen. Sometimes they are planted solely for their nitrogen content.

A vegetable plate is a favorite in our household, and especially at the beginning of harvest season. A vegetable plate is just not complete without some type of beans such as crowder peas, black-eyed peas, or butter beans. It has always been a favorite family tradition to spend the afternoon on the porch shelling peas to "put up" for the winter. Now with our big family, the peas rarely make it to the "put up" stage, but nonetheless, shelling peas is timeless and is enjoyed by every generation and should be a time for celebration!

Butter Beans

Serves 8

Ingredients

2 tablespoons olive oil
½ cup Vidalia onion, chopped
1 clove garlic, minced
1 pound butter beans
2 okra, whole
4 cups chicken stock
1 teaspoon kosher salt
¼ teaspoon freshly ground pepper
½ lemon, juiced
1 tablespoon butter
3 tablespoons sliced green onion tops (green part)

Heat olive oil in medium saucepan over medium-high heat. Add the onions and reduce heat to medium until onions are translucent. Add the garlic and cook for 1 minute.

Add the beans, okra, stock, salt, pepper, lemon juice and butter. Bring to a boil. Reduce the heat and simmer for 25 - 30 minutes or until the beans are tender. Be careful to keep an eye on the beans. Add water if they look dry. Season as desired. Serve with sliced green onions.

Herbs: Grow and Cook with The Original Medicine

Herbs,

When I think about herbs, my mind automatically thinks of the words beautiful, fragrant, and tasty, but herbs go much deeper than that. Throughout all of history people have used herbs medicinally as an antiseptic, antibiotic, or even as a relaxant. Herbs have many functions and can grow easily just about anywhere. Herbs can be grown indoors in pots and outdoors in the ground as a shrub or a pot by the door. If nothing else tempts you to grow your own herbs, the mere fact that your food will begin to taste like a 5 star restaurant with the simple use of fresh herbs should suffice. The one drawback is that you may never want to eat out again!

Herbs grown indoors need at least 6 hours of sunlight. I do not have windows in my kitchen, but I have large porches for containers, a designated spot between 2 sets of stairs right off the porch near the kitchen, and an herb garden for growing herbs. I love to mix edible flowers in with my herbs as well as plant herbs as shrubbery.

I have planted rosemary foundation plants and have layered other herbs such as lemongrass, basil, oregano, thyme, and sage intermixed with flowers for about 2 feet into the yard. I love to border with my beloved strawberries. These herbs are incredibly easy to grow and I adore the untamed look of all of them growing together.

This year I have planted an Italian Herb Pot and an old fountain with onions and parsley. Not only are they beautiful and functional, they make it easy for the small children to collect the herbs to go on my Quail Pizza! The Italian Herb Pot consists of basil, Italian parsley, marjoram, sage, rosemary and thyme.

The key to healthy herbs is to keep them moist. If you live in a dry climate mist your herbs often. Herbs also love to be harvested often for optimal health and productivity of the plant. Don't forget to dry or freeze your herbs! Enjoy a fantastic culinary experience!

Herb Frittata

Serves 4 – 6

This recipe reminds me of spring mornings and is one of the first recipes that I make when my herb garden begins to bloom. I would grow herbs just for this frittata!!

Ingredients

8 large eggs
2 teaspoons Kosher salt
½ teaspoon freshly ground pepper
2 tablespoons fresh thyme, chopped
2 tablespoon sage leaves, chopped
½ cup Italian parsley leaves, chopped
½ cup fresh basil leaves, chopped
1 shallot, diced
1 cup mozzarella cheese, shredded
4 tablespoons butter

Place rack in oven close to the broiler and set broiler on high. In a large bowl, blend eggs with salt and pepper until frothy. Add thyme, sage, parsley, basil, shallots, and cheese to egg mixture and blend.

In an 8 to 10-inch sauté pan, heat butter until it begins to bubble. Add the egg mixture and cook over medium-heat for 5 minutes or until it is set on the bottom and sides of pan. Transfer pan to the oven and broil for about 3 minutes or until the eggs are puffed and lightly browned. Sprinkle with parsley and serve.

Herb Salad *with* Simple Vinaigrette

Serves 4–6

Herb salad is the epitome of freshness. It reminds me of those beautiful 75-degree days that we rarely see in Alabama. This light and refreshing salad would be perfect for a brunch.

Ingredients: Salad

4 cups lettuce mix
¼ cup parsley leaves
¼ cup chives, cut into 1 inch pieces
¼ cup mint leaves
½ cup edible flowers
½ cup vinaigrette

Ingredients: Simple Vinaigrette

3 tablespoons salad vinegar
6 tablespoons olive oil
½ teaspoon Kosher salt
¼ teaspoon freshly ground pepper

In a small bowl, add vinegar. Slowly whisk oil into vinegar mixing constantly to form an emulsion. Add salt and pepper.

Combine lettuce, herbs and flowers in a medium sized bowl. Stir in about ¼ cup Simple Vinaigrette. Gently combine. Drizzle with extra vinaigrette as desired.

All flowers in the rose family are edible as well as impatiens, pansies, marigolds, dandelions, and goldenrod.

Herb Balsamic Vinaigrette

Yields about 1 ½ cups

This vinaigrette is made with several of the most healthful foods known to man. It is especially great served over cabbage, fish, or turkey and for dipping raw or cooked vegetables. Do not forget to drizzle over breads and pizza as well.

Balsamic Vinegar is filled with anti-oxidants and contains Pepsin which improves the bodies metabolism.

Ingredients

½ cup balsamic vinegar
2 tablespoons honey
1 teaspoon Dijon mustard
1 teaspoon Kosher salt
Freshly ground pepper to taste
2 teaspoons fresh basil, finely chopped
2 teaspoons fresh parsley, chopped
2 teaspoons fresh oregano, chopped
1 cup olive oil

Mix first 8 ingredients in a large bowl. Slowly pour olive oil into mixture while continuously whisking to ensure an emulsion.

Basil, The Holy Herb

Sweet Basil, sometimes known as Saint Joseph's Wort, is typically found in Italian Cuisine, but there are other varieties that are excellent as well including lemon, cinnamon, and Thai Basil. Basil is also known as the "king of herbs" or as the "holy herb". Basil truly is a fascinating and healthy herb. It contains flavonoids, which protect cell structure and chromosomes from radiation and oxygen based damage and well as being full of Vitamin A and Vitamin K.

Basil is incredibly easy to grow. It grows just about anywhere including the cracks between the bricks in my walkway. Of course, I do live in Basil's favorite environment. Basil loves hot, dry environments. If you live in a cold environment, basil will grow well in a pot placed near a Southern facing window. Let it dry out completely, then water it.

To promote more growth, pick the leaves often. Once the basil is allowed to flower, you can save the small black seeds and plant them the following year.

Basil Pesto

Yields 1 Cup

Basil Pesto is incredibly versatile. I like to serve it over hot noodles, with Eggplant Parmesan, fried squash or over eggs.

Ingredients

¼ cup pine nuts
3 cloves garlic
½ teaspoon Kosher salt
½ teaspoon freshly ground black pepper
¾ cup olive oil
2½ cups basil leaves
1 cup Romano cheese

In a food processor fitted with the steel blade, place pine nuts, garlic, basil, Romano, salt and pepper. Slowly feed olive oil through feed tube of processor and process until pureed.

To freeze:

Line an ice cube tray with plastic wrap, and fill each pocket with pesto.

Freeze and remove from tray and store in freezer bag. When ready to use, defrost and add cheese. Freeze for up to 3 months.

Place a thin layer of olive oil over pesto and store pesto in refrigerator. It will keep it from browning.

If you are going to freeze, omit the cheese and add after the pesto has thawed. Because the cheese is omitted, the pesto will be a bit runny; it will thicken once you thaw and process with cheese.

Basil is used as an insect repellant for us and our gardens!

Preserving Summer: Can, Freeze, and Dry Your Harvest

Oh yes, you can do this. All you have to do is be prepared and have the right tools available and plenty of fresh fruits and vegetables. Almost anything can be preserved in some kind of way, either, by canning, freezing or drying.

People think that canning or drying foods is scary and difficult, but just the opposite; it is healthy and easy. When you can, dry, and freeze the produce you have grown, you know absolutely everything that has gone into those vegetables and fruits. You are taking charge of your own health and food. Not only are you taking charge of your family's health and the food that they eat, you are working together as a family for a common good and enjoying relationships that will last for a lifetime, not to mention extra money for any surplus that you may sell. Every year my family sells canned figs, mint jellies, and other preserves at an upscale arts and crafts show in our community. We sell a lot of different items, but the canned preserves are always the first to go and at a high price too!

CANNING

There are two main approaches to canning; the boiling water canning method and the pressure canning method. Fruits and tomatoes may be processed using the boiling water method found below, but the United States Department of Agriculture recommends that the pressure canner method is the only safe method for canning low acid foods such as vegetables, poultry and meats. If using the pressure canner method, always be sure to follow instructions in your manual. The steps will be the same as the boiling method of canning up until you place the jars into the canner.

Boiling Method

First, you need to gather the tools that you will need for preserving.

~large stockpot
~ladle
~funnel
~tongs (with coated handles) for lifting jars
~glass canning jars
~magnetic lid lifter
~lids
~bands
~saucepan for sterilizing lids
~clean dish towels

These can be bought at you local supermarket as a 9~ or 12~piece canning kit.

Step 1

Sterilize

Be organized and prepared before beginning. Always, always read your recipe carefully and thoroughly, and gather all of your equipment and ingredients. Make sure all equipment is in good condition, no broken or cracked jars or rusted bands. Always use new lids. Place glass jars in a large stockpot covered with water. Bring the water to a boil and continue to boil for 10 minutes. As you are ready to fill the jars, lift them out carefully with the jar lifter, emptying the water. Place these sterilized jars on a clean surface that will not scorch or burn. A clean dish towel, butcher paper or paper towels will do just fine. Quick tip—the sterilization option on your dishwasher will more than adequately handle the sterilization process.

Bring a small saucepan of water to a simmer and remove from heat. Drop the jar lids into the saucepan, cover the pan and let lids warm for at least 10 minutes. The lids should not be removed until the jars are ready to be sealed. A magnetic lid lifter makes it easier to remove the lids from the pan.

The jars and lids are now sterilized.

Step 2

Prepare recipe, seal, and process

Prepare the recipe as directed. Ladle the mixture into the sterilized jars leaving ½ inch air space at the top. Remove all bubbles, wipe excess mixture from the threads of the jars, place sterilized lid on each jar using a magnetic lid lifter. Screw the bands onto the jars securely. Immediately, place the jars into the canning rack. Boil the jars in water 2-3 inches over the top of the jars. Keep the water at that level and boiling until you have reached the specified processing time. Times will vary depending on sizes of jars and ingredients. Let the jars cool in the canner for a few minutes and then remove. Place processed jars on a kitchen towel and allow cooling for 12-24 hours. These may be stored for up to one year or longer.

If you are preparing a recipe low in acid, you will need to use the Pressure Canning Method. All of the steps of canning are the same until the water is placed inside the canner. If Pressure Canning, place 2 to 3 inches of water in the canner, then place the rack and jars inside being careful not to allow the jars to touch each other or the sides of the canner. Snap the lid closed. Allow steam to come out of the canner for 10 minutes. Place the correct weight on the vent to pressurize the canner (the correct weight will be given in your canner instruction manual). Begin timing when the weight starts to wiggle or the gauge reads the correct pressure. Keep the heat as even as possible and when the time is up remove canner from heat. Allow the pressure to return to zero and release the steam. Open lid and direct steam away from you. Remove jars and place on a rack or kitchen towel and allow to slowly cool.

If lids do not "pop" down or you notice that the middle of the lid gives under pressure, place in the refrigerator and enjoy for a few months. These jars did not process properly.

Do not forget to label and date. Personalize your creations with labels, pieces of cloth and ribbons. You will love these as you begin to use them – they might even be given for gifts, or taken to parties. ENJOY!!!!

FREEZING

Freezing is a great way to preserve your harvest. This is my favorite way to preserve meat as well as many vegetables and fruits.

Freezing meat is a "must" for those of you buying whole cows or those that hunt large game. Meat can be canned and dried, but freezing saves room and allows for more options in cooking. After allowing freshly harvested meat such as poultry, wild game, or recently butchered beef to age, wrap in airtight, moisture proof containers. Of course, there are vacuum sealers that are an excellent way to freeze meats. There are freezer jars and plastic containers, but my favorite is freezer paper. It saves room and is easy to label. There are great instructions that come with the freezer paper. I like to double wrap the meat to insure freshness. Always thaw your meat in the refrigerator when ready to use the meat.

When freezing fruit, I have found it best not to wash the fruit, but to brush any visible debris from the fruit instead. Washing the fruit tends to make it mushy upon thawing. Take your harvest and freeze individually on a cookie sheet. Once frozen, grab a freezer bag and fill it with your frozen fruit and place back into freezer. It is as easy as that!

When freezing fresh vegetables, always clean them, check them carefully for dirt, or other debris. Once they are clean, the next step is blanching. Blanching consists of boiling the raw vegetables for 2-3 minutes and then stopping the blanching process by cooling. Cooling is accomplished either by placing the vegetables immediately into cool to cold water. This completely stops the cooking process and the vegetables are then ready to be placed in freezer bags or containers and frozen until you are ready to enjoy them.

DRYING

Drying is perhaps the oldest method of preserving. It dates back to the days of our ancient ancestors and Native Americans. They preserved their harvests long before canners, pressure cookers, and freezers were invented. They sun-dried their fruits and vegetables, but I prefer using the oven. I do not have to deal with insects that way! It is easy to dry fruits, vegetables, herbs, and even chili peppers. You more than likely already have all that is needed to pursue preservation by this method.

Drying Beans and Peppers

1. Wash your harvest and string your beans, peppers, and herbs together with a needle and heavy-duty thread or fishing line, making a knot around each bean.
2. Repeat until the thread is full and then simply hang these beans for several months in a dry place.

Drying Fruits and Vegetables

One of my favorite methods of drying is that of using the oven or a dehydrator. My children especially love preserving their harvest by this method. They love making dried fruits such as peaches, apples, figs, and berries. I love them preserving using the drying method as they eat these delicious fruits and berries as snacks rather than all of the snacks chocked full of sugars and artificial ingredients that seem to have made their way into our diets at the grocery stores. Preserving really offers us a much healthier way of living our lives. If using a dehydrator, follow the instructions in your manual.

Drying using Oven

1. Set the oven to the lowest possible setting.
2. Slice your fruits and vegetables into thin pieces and place on a cookie sheet.
3. Cook overnight or until all moisture is removed.
4. Store your dried goods, pack them in freezer bags or in food-saver packets. Freeze them for up to a year.

JERKY

And, let's not forget jerky. My men love their jerky. After they have prepared the finer venison for the freezer, they use the less desired meat for jerky. The result is another wonderfully healthy snack loaded with protein.

1. Heat the oven to 200 degrees.
2. Thinly slice meat and season as you desire.
3. Place meat about 1/2 inch apart on a cookie sheet.
4. Bake for six hours.

Fig Preserves

2 pints

Ingredients

1 pound fresh ripe figs
1 cup sugar
2 tablespoons lemon juice

Combine figs, sugar, and lemon juice together in a medium-sized saucepan and cook on low heat for 30 minutes uncovered.

Process 10 minutes using the boiling method as described on page 116.

Homemade Biscuits

Serves 8–12

Keep shortening in freezer to keep cold

Ingredients

3 cups flour plus enough for dusting
1 tablespoon baking powder
½ teaspoon baking soda
¾ teaspoon salt
½ cup (1 stick) butter, cold
3 tablespoons shortening, cold
1 cup buttermilk

Preheat oven to 425 degrees.

In a large bowl, mix dry ingredients together.

Cut butter into pea-size pieces. Work shortening and butter into the dry ingredients until incorporated. It should resemble an oatmeal texture. Be careful not to over mix or the texture will be affected.

Pour buttermilk into mixture. Place dough onto lightly floured surface and fold on top of itself for about 1 minute. Roll dough to 1½ inch thickness. Cut into 3 to 4 inch rounds.

Place on silpat or greased cookie sheet. Make sure the biscuits are touching each other. Put a light thumbprint in center of each biscuit to keep them even when rising.

Place in oven for 20 minutes or until golden brown. Halfway through baking lightly brush with melted butter and bake for the remaining 10 minutes. Serve immediately.

Homemade Canned Tomatoes

I use canned tomatoes for a good portion of my recipes. In my opinion, tomatoes give flavor that no other vegetable can give. In the summer, it is like a factory in my kitchen as we can tomatoes day and night so as not to let even one of our precious tomatoes over-ripen. As a diversion, we prepare and snack on salsa while we continue our vigil of canning.

1. Drop tomatoes in boiling water for about 20 seconds. Remove from hot water. Remove skin from tomatoes by cutting ends off and squeezing from bottom.
2. Push down into a sterilized Mason jar. Add 2 teaspoons of lemon juice. Fasten lid tightly.
3. Submerge Mason jar in water. Bring to a boil and continue boiling for 40 minutes for pint-sized jars and 45 minutes for quart-sized jars.

Once opened, keep refrigerated. They should last in refrigerator for a couple of weeks.

Fresh Salsa

This salsa requires fresh vine ripe vegetables to get the full flavor I enjoy so much. As soon as my vegetables are ripe, I bring them in and make this perfect sweet and spicy salsa!

Place a bowl upside down over the roasted vegetables for 5 minutes while allowing them to cool. It will make peeling them easier.

Ingredients

5 medium-size tomatoes (½ pound)
2 jalapeño chilies
2 cloves garlic
1 red bell pepper
1 lime, juiced
1 tablespoon olive oil
1 tablespoon cilantro
1 teaspoon Kosher salt

Preheat oven to 500 degrees. Core the tomatoes and half lengthwise. Place the tomatoes cut-side down in a lined cookie sheet. Add the whole jalapeño and bell pepper on the cookie sheet and roast for 7-10 minutes, or until skin is charred. Turn peppers occasionally.

When cool, remove skin from vegetables plus the seeds from the peppers and place in food processor. Add remaining ingredients to a food processor.

Pulse food processor until almost smooth. Serve immediately or refrigerate for up to 1 week. If canning, use pressure canning method and refer to pressure canner instruction manual for this recipe.

Tomatillo Sauce

Pick tomatillos at the peak of freshness, when yellow, for best flavor.

Ingredients

10 medium-sized tomatillos (2 ounces), husk removed, cored, and cut in half lengthwise.
1 jalapeño chili
1 Vidalia or yellow onion, quartered
2 cloves garlic
3 tablespoons fresh cilantro
1 lime, juiced
Salt and pepper to taste

Preheat oven to 500 degrees. Place tomatillos cut side up and whole jalapeños on a baking sheet and roast for 7–10 minutes or until black spots appear on tomatillos. Turn baking sheet halfway through roasting process.

When cool, remove as much skin as possible from vegetables along with the seeds and stem of jalapeño chili. Place in food processor. Add onions, garlic, cilantro, and lime juice and puree to the consistency of your liking. Season liberally with salt and add pepper to taste.

Serve immediately or refrigerate for up to a week. If canning, use pressure canning method and refer to pressure canner instruction manual for this recipe.

Drying Figs

1. Set your oven on the lowest setting. It is probably around 135 degrees.

2. Remove stems, cut figs in half, and lay them flesh side up on the cookie sheet turning occasionally for 24 hours or until the outsides are leathery and there are no juices when you put pressure on the figs. Keep the oven door slightly open so that the figs dry instead of cook. You can do this in 12-hour cycles by turning the oven off during the night if you choose.

3. Store figs in an air-tight container for several months. Figs will last in the freezer up to 24 months.

Drying figs in a food dehydrator will work equally as well. Follow the manufacturer's instructions.

Granny's Garden Vegetable Soup

My grandmother was one of the best Southern cooks I have ever known and my dad is one of the best gardeners I know. The pair could make a mean soup! I could live on this soup forever!

Adding freshly squeezed lemon always brightens a dish!

Ingredients

3 tablespoons olive oil
2 celery stalks, chopped
1 large onion, chopped
1 clove garlic, crushed
2 pounds okra, sliced into ¼ inch thick rounds
8–10 tomatoes, peeled and crushed
¾ cup butter beans
4 ears of corn (1 cup), cut off the cob
1 tablespoon basil, chopped
1 tablespoon thyme, chopped
3 dashes of hot sauce
1 tablespoon salt
½ teaspoon pepper
1 lemon

In a large stockpot, heat olive oil over medium heat. Add celery, onions, and garlic and heat for about 1 minute stirring constantly.

Add okra, tomatoes, beans, corn, basil, thyme, hot sauce, salt, and pepper to the pot. Squeeze the lemon over soup. Add enough water to just cover the soup.

Bring mixture to a boil, and then reduce to simmer. Cover and let simmer for 1 hour.

Enjoy now with Jalapeño Cornbread (page 56) or use pressure canner method of canning to can this recipe.

Beyond the Garden

In The Field!!

Foraging:

Wild Fruits, Herbs, and Greens

Foraging or "living off the land" as my kids like to call it, is one of our family's favorite hobbies...or should I say adventures. There is something so special about being out in God's creation, picking the plants and herbs He provides for us, and making meals from what we harvest. One of my favorite things is being able to snack on the things I have just picked. There is nothing more organic than that!

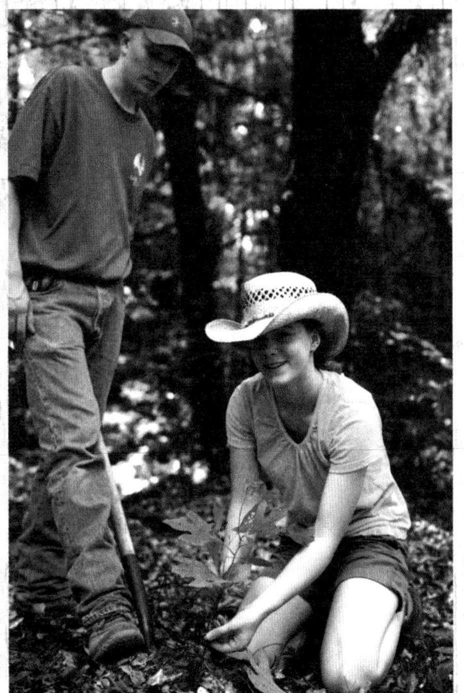

All of us have a natural foraging instinct that cannot be quenched in a grocery store shopping experience. Even though many health markets are offering wild herbs, and vegetables such as dandelion greens and wood sorrel, there is nothing like being out in the fresh air and picking it yourself. We love to go on hikes each spring on a berry expedition and competition. Whoever fills their bags the fastest with wild berries gets the first piece of the homemade pie made from the berries.

When I was younger, my dad would take me to visit my cousins who live way out in the "country". They had a great big crab apple tree next to a trampoline, and I thought it was the greatest thing that we could just pick a snack off the tree and lay down on the trampoline and eat until our heart's desire. Every child, or adult for that matter, needs this kind of rest and recreation in the wild open world. Seeing my children picking crab apples off the tree or eating ripe persimmons and muscadines reminds me of those sweet childhood memories.

Some of our very favorite plants to forage are sassafras and purslane. There is an overgrown road behind our house that grows sassafras trees profusely. Sassafras was one of the largest imports from America second only to tobacco in the 1600s.

We use it as a thickener in soups and gumbo as well as tea. The sassafras adds a slight licorice taste to the tea and gives root beer its licorice flavor.

Our farm, in Central Alabama is full of purslane. It is a leafy vegetable in which stems, leaves, and flower buds are edible. Purslane has the highest amount of Omega 3 fatty acids of any vegetable. We use purslane in salad as well as sauté them for a bed underneath fish in that their tangy flavor enhances in much the same way as lemon or lime.

The nutritional value of wild herbs and fruits are amazingly high compared to their domestic counterpart. Wild berries such as blackberries, huckleberries, elder berries, and dewberries contain more of the powerful antioxidant anthocyanin as well as taste tangier and sweeter than domestic berries. Anthocyanin is believed to protect against brain aging and vision health. Fruits and berries are nature's candy. A crab apple has twice the fiber as regular apples. There are just a few examples of the extraordinary benefit of eating wild.

Our ancestors "lived off the land" whether they hunted, raised, or gathered their food. There is a satisfaction and a great reward for harvesting wild proteins, herbs, vegetables, and fruits for yourself. Not only do you feel accomplished, but also you save money, eat healthier, and enjoy the taste of the freshest foods you can have. We enjoy the process of surviving off the land and making use of the great bounty found in nature. We hope that you and your family will enjoy it as much as we do.

The extremely invasive vine, Kudzu, was consumed during famines in Japan and saved many lives. Not only is Kudzu higher in calories than most herbs, it increases circulation to reduce pain and stiffness, and has been used as a beta blocker for racing pulse induced by stress.

Dandelion Greens, Wood Sorrel, Greenbrier, *and* Turkey *with* Balsamic Herb Vinaigrette

Serves 4

Dandelions have been attributed to curing liver disease, prevent and cure high blood pressure, prevent various forms of cancer and assist in weight reduction. On top of being delicious, this meal is inevitably healthy. Most folks could walk right into their backyard and have a nutritious meal on the table within minutes!

Dandelions have been used in anti-plaque preparations by dental researchers.

Ingredients

3 cups dandelion greens
⅓ cup greenbrier
⅓ cup wood sorrel
⅓ cup green onions
¼ cup mulberries
¼ cup strawberries
1 cup Herb Balsamic Vinaigrette (page 110)
1 pound turkey breast, sliced into 1 inch slices
2 tablespoons olive oil
1 tablespoon Kosher salt
1 teaspoon freshly ground pepper

In a large bowl, place ½ cup of the Herb Balsamic Vinaigrette. Gently mix dandelion greens, greenbrier, wood sorrel, onions, mulberries, strawberries with the Vinaigrette and divide greens among 4 plates.

Pound each turkey slice to about ⅛ inch thick and cut into bite sized pieces.

In a medium-sized bowl, mix olive oil, salt, pepper and turkey pieces together.

Heat cast iron skillet to almost smoking and cook turkey pieces in batches for 2 minutes on each side. Be sure not to crowd the pan so that your meat browns and does not steam.

Divide turkey pieces among the four salad plates. Drizzle a little Herb Balsamic Vinaigrette over the salad as desired. Serve with your favorite Crusty Bread.

Greenbrier is available in most super markets. If you cannot find it just add more Dandelion Greens. Greenbrier is in the smilax family which is most notable for providing sarsaparilla found in root beer, and it is rumored that the smilax steroid treats dementia and Alzheimer's patients.

Blueberry Pie

One of my favorite times of the year is late spring when all of our wild blueberries are ripe. Our family tradition is to see who can pick the most berries. Mary, my eight year old, won this year, but I think it is due to her self-control. Everyone else was digging into their stash and she saved every one of hers. We come home, announce winners, make this awesome Wild Blueberry Pie and give the first slice to the winner. I hope this tradition lasts through the generations.

Ingredients

2 homemade pie crusts (page 48)
5 ½ cups blueberries
⅓ cup brown sugar
⅓ cup granulated sugar, plus 2 tablespoons for sprinkling
1 teaspoon cinnamon
¼ cup flour, plus 2 tablespoons for sprinkling
1 large egg, beaten
1 tablespoon heavy cream

You can substitute domestic cultivated berries in the pie if wild berries are not in season.

Brushing the top lattice with heavy cream or an egg and sprinkling raw sugar on the tops of the lattice crust gives it a prettier appearance as well as a nice crunch.

Preheat oven to 375 degrees.

In a large bowl combine berries, brown sugar, granulated sugar, cinnamon and flour. Stir gently.

Sprinkle 2 tablespoons of flour and 2 tablespoons of granulated sugar on the bottom of chilled crust. Pour filling into the crust, follow lattice crust instructions page 43 and bake in oven for one hour or until blueberries are bubbly and crust is golden. Serve with ice cream or homemade whipped cream.

The sassafras tree has been historically a very important tree. At one point in the 1600's it was one of the largest imports from America, second only to tobacco. The Creole and the Cajuns learned from the Indians the thickening qualities of sassafras leaves and it soon became part of their cuisine. The roots of the tree became the key ingredient in the original root beer or could be made into a delightful tea.

Our family loves sassafras tea; there is nothing quite like it. The only way I can describe the taste is something like a fruity licorice drink. If you want to make this classic tea, then follow the simple recipe below.

Sassafras Tea

Makes 1 Gallon

If you have your own property, or permission of a landowner, walk along the sides of the roads and look for 3-5ft sassafras sapling. They are quite easy to spot by their leaves; all the leaves are toothless with varying lobe shapes.

Once located, slowly ease the tree up by pulling as low down on the tree as you can, trying to recover as much of the tap root as possible (You might have to loosen the soil with a shovel).

Take a pair of garden sheers and cut the root away from the trunk. Keep the top of the tree if you plan on making filé. Wash the roots well.

Weigh out 2 oz. of root and cut into 1-inch pieces.

Place the root pieces strait into a pot of water and bring to a simmer. Let simmer for 5-minutes then let cool for another 10-minutes for maximum flavor.

Meanwhile, measure 1½-cups of sugar and place in a gallon pitcher.

Set a cheese-clothe over the pitcher and fasten it with a rubber band.

Pour in the tea and dissolve sugar.

Chill and serve iced. ENJOY!

Now you are left with a bunch of sassafras tree tops. In Louisiana the Creole and the Cajuns make a killer gumbo using powdered sassafras leaves they call filé powder. Here is how to make this southern thickener.

Filé Powder

Preparation:

Bundle several sassafras branches and hang in your attic, basement,or garage. It is best to keep it in a dark, dry environment.

When dry, remove leaves and place in a food processor. Chop until a very fine powder, about 2 minutes.

Sift the filé powder to rid it of stem bases. Place in a airtight container and store in a cool, dark place. It should keep a year.

You can use filé powder in gumbo and soups in place of roux or okra. Just slowly add until you have desired consistency. The flavor of the filé itself is light but has a slight earthy taste that adds richness and body to the dish. It can also be used as a final garnish.

Bon appetite!

Have you ever had Kudzu (yes, kudzu) jelly? I had the opportunity this winter to have one of my son's professor's of cell biology, Dr. Robert Estes, over for dinner. He and his wife, Melinda, brought such hospitality with them in the form of jelly...Kudzu jelly. I couldn't wait to open it and have it on crackers. I just love jelly on crackers – the salt brings out the flavor in the jelly. Amazingly, it tasted sweet and a little floral. Truly, it may be one of my favorite jellies.

Did you know that Kudzu is used to treat migraine headaches, Alzheimer's Disease, and hangovers? It's got an amazing amount of anti-inflammatory properties and antimicrobial properties. It's also used to make soap, paper, and clothing.

Although Kudzu is highly invasive, it's uses are quite plentiful as well as it's high calories in times of famine. It has been used often in Japan in times of emergency and famine. Go get yourself some Kudzu today and enjoy!!

Kudzu Jelly

Ingredients

4 cups kudzu gently pressed blossoms
4 cups water
Juice of ½ lemon
8 cups sugar
2 packs liquid pectin

Rinse kudzu blossoms in cold water. In a medium saucepan, bring 4 cups of water to a boil then reduce to simmer for about 15 minutes. Remove blossoms from the heat and allow to cool.

Strain the blossoms over cheesecloth into another saucepan. Add ½ to 1 cup of water to the blossom water to bring the amount back up to 4 cups. Return the remaining liquid to the stove, and lemon juice and cook over high heat until the mixture reaches 220 degrees. Add the pectin and bring mixture back up to a boil for another 2 minutes. Skim the top, if necessary, and proceed to the boiling method of canning (page 114).

Beekeeping and Honey:
Live the Sweet Life

Live Bees
This Side Up

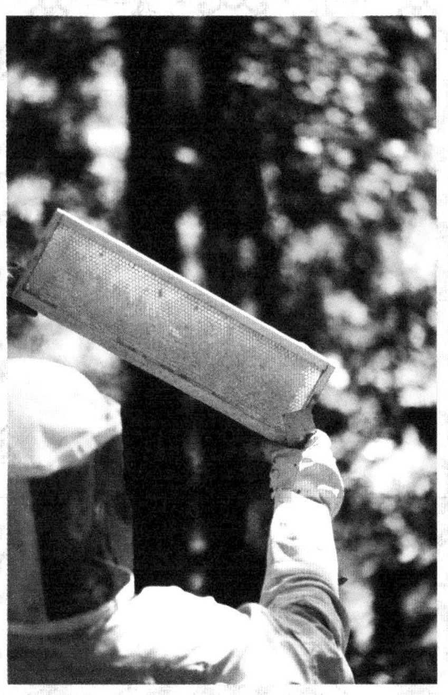

Solomon, the wisest man in the world, said these wise words to his son, "My son, eat thou honey, because it is good, and the honeycomb is sweet to thy taste." Bees have been a huge part of history and culture from the beginning of time. One of the earliest noted references of a beekeeper was around 3000 BC whereby a beekeeper near the Nile River begged for someone to send his donkeys to transport his hives before the flood demolished them.

Honey has been and is still today a treasured commodity associated with health and prosperity. In the book of Exodus, the Israelites were promised to dwell in a land "flowing with milk and honey." There is no greater sweetener in the world and the health benefits are amazing.

I must admit that upon the bee's arrival, I was a little apprehensive. It did not take me very long to learn to love them though. They gently let you know when you are being intrusive by racing toward you and slamming into your forehead. I can't lie; my stomach still drops and I get a rush of adrenaline when this "warning" from my bees occur. The kids love tending to the hives as if they are our pets, and kind of they are. They work very hard for us collecting pollen and making loads of honey. I see appreciation from the kids as they nurture and protect these wonderful honey bees.

It seems that the medicinal, culinary, and household uses of honey and wax are endless. Honey needs little digestion giving a quick energy boost without the crash of white sugar and other carbohydrates. Honey is known as an antiseptic, sleep aid, immunity booster, anti-inflammatory, circulation increaser, in addition to being the main component in a tincture to stave off colds or treat a sore throat. Bee stings have been known to manage pain in arthritic patients and a tablespoon of local honey taken once a day will eradicate allergy symptoms.

Bees are a gardener's best friend in that 80% of all pollination that takes place is done by bees. Gardener's have better productivity of fruits, flowers, and vegetables. Wild life also benefit from greater amounts of clover fields, fruit trees, fruit bearing bushes, and wild herbs and plants.

Bee's wax contributes to many households in the form of beautiful and natural furniture wax, water repellant, and candles.

I am ever so thankful to the colonists for importing bees to the United States in the 1600's. Our gardens have better yield, our food has better flavor, or bodies are healthier, and our skin ages less rapidly when using products with honey in them. The benefits of beekeeping far outweigh the time involved. It only takes about an hour a week and 1 day twice a year to harvest the honey. Your yield will be well worth it as well as the benefit to the community. If you do not have time to devote to beekeeping, please support your local beekeepers.

If you are interested in beekeeping contact your local Beekeeper's Association. There are many beekeeping supply companies that can help you get started as well. They will supply you with protective clothing, hives, tools, and bees. Bees are like caring for any other special pet. They need protection from the elements, water, food, and lots of love and appreciation!

You are more likely to get stung on a cloudy, windy, or rainy day. Almost all commercial bees are treated with various chemicals and medications.

Did You Know?

One worker bee will visit 100 flowers per collection trip but only make ½ tablespoon of honey in a lifetime.

It takes 2 million flowers pollinated to produce one jar of honey.

Honey helps burn fat while you sleep.

1 Tablespoon of honey taken 4 times a day relieves pain in stomach ulcers.

Honey will store indefinitely. Honey has been found in Egyptian tombs dating back 3,300 years ago and in great condition.

Cinnamon Pear Buns are a cross between cinnamon buns and homemade apple pie. These two American comfort foods combined together are a delight at any breakfast table or even for dessert. Because there is no yeast in this recipe, they are quick and easy to make. I also love the fact that I get pears, oranges, and honey all in one bite. If you have left over Honey Bourbon Sauce, it makes for a great ice cream topping!

Ingredients

2 cups all-purpose flour
4 teaspoons baking powder
½ teaspoon salt
¼ cup shortening
¾ cup buttermilk
2 pears, diced
½ cup sugar
1 teaspoon cinnamon
½ stick melted butter
(4 tablespoons)

Honey bourbon sauce

1½ cup honey
2 tablespoons cornstarch
juice of 1 orange
3 tablespoons bourbon
⅛ teaspoon salt

Cinnamon Pear Buns with Honey Bourbon Sauce

Preheat oven to 400 degrees.

In a large bowl, mix flour, baking powder, and salt.

Work the shortening into the dry ingredients quickly with your hands then add the buttermilk without overworking.

In a small bow, mix sugar and cinnamon.

Roll dough out to ¼ inch thick rectangle. Cover the rectangle with the diced pears leaving a ½ inch border around the edges and sprinkle the cinnamon sugar mixture on top of the pears. Beginning at the end farthest from you(this should be the long end of the roll), roll the rectangle towards you then cut the log into eight 1 inch slices.

Butter a baking dish and place the cinnamon rolls into the dish. Distribute the melted butter equally over the top of the buns and place them in the oven for 20-25 minutes or until golden brown.

Meanwhile, prepare the bourbon sauce by combining the honey, juice of one orange, bourbon, and salt in a small saucepan. Heat sauce over medium heat and reduce by about a third. This should take 10 minutes. Stir mixture often.

Remove the buns from the oven and serve with warm sauce.

Honey Butter Sauce

Yields about ¾ cup

This sauce is great with waffles, pancakes, pound cakes, biscuits, and even over ice cream!

Ingredients

¼ cup butter, melted
¼ cup honey
¼ cup orange juice
½ teaspoon vanilla

In a medium-sized bowl, mix melted butter, honey, orange juice, and vanilla until well blended and smooth.

Baked Peaches with Honey *and* Almonds

Serves 8

Peaches are the epitome of summer in the south. About 20 miles north of our home is the peach capital of Alabama. There are several local peach farms that sell these juicy ripe peaches to peach markets located right by US I-65 in between Montgomery and Birmingham. Travelers must stop by and try their fabulously perfected peach ice cream. I love to devour peaches right off the tree from our yard, but as a special easy treat for the family, I love to make this recipe. The crunch and flavor of the almonds play perfectly with this decadent fruit!

Peaches are rich in vitamin A, Beta-carotene as well as potassium, fluoride, and iron. Peaches actually prevent tooth decay.

Ingredients

4 tablespoons butter
4 peaches halved, cored, and skinned
8 tablespoons skinned almonds
8 tablespoons honey

Preheat oven to 350 degrees. Place butter in bottom of casserole and melt butter.

Place peaches core-side up in baking dish.

In a small bowl, combine almonds and honey. Divide the honey mixture among the peaches. Bake in oven for 25 minutes or until peaches pierce easily with a knife. Serve with ice cream or whipped cream.

Melon Salad with Honey Poppy Seed Dressing

Ingredients

2 cups honeydew melon
2 cups muskmelon (cantaloupe)
2 cups watermelon
1 tablespoon mint, chopped

Honey Poppyseed Dressing:

1½ cup olive oil
½ cup honey
⅓ cup salad vinegar
2 tablespoons Dijon mustard
2 tablespoons poppy seed
½ teaspoon salt

Cut melons in half. Scoop out seeds with spoon and discard.

With a melon ball scooper or mini ice cream scooper, scoop 1-inch balls and place in large bowl. Remove seeds from watermelon as you scoop.

In a food processor, mix all of the dressing ingredients until thick and emulsified. Stir in mint.

Pour ¼ of the dressing over the fruit and coat the melons thoroughly. Store the remaining dressing in the refrigerator for up to 2 weeks.

Poultry and Eggs: Chicken, Turkey, and Eggs

Fun, beautiful, and perfect! That is how I feel about chickens. They are extremely smart and have very distinct, wonderful (at least most of the time) personalities. Since the chick's arrival our family has laughed chasing them around the yard, watching them strut, and listening to the roosters, which we did not know we had, show their dominance. They have produced the best eggs I have ever eaten and been a friend and entertainment for my six year old daughter.

Scott and the kids had been talking for some time about raising chickens, but I really did not take them too seriously. They are always dreaming and planning something. One morning I woke up to banging and saw noises. They boys were creating a chicken tractor for the new baby chicks! Sure enough the post office called and said that I needed to pick up a box that was making a lot of noise. That was the beginning of our chicken adventure!

I certainly did not know what to do with these adorable baby chicks, but Scott and the kids had done the research. We set up a heating lamp in a large cage filled with hay and supplied with water and food on our front porch. It was our own homemade brooder. At the end of the day the entire family went to bed with a feeling of accomplishment and the excitement of a new adventure... except me. I lay wide awake worrying that the 6 chicks would be too hot or too cold, or that the heating lamp would burn them somehow. I was already forming a motherly instinct toward them!

The chickens grew like children...that is like weeds! Five months passed and we got our first gorgeous light blue egg from our Ameraucana. They continued to lay eggs until winter when we noticed that we were only getting approximately one egg a week. The days were shorter and the chickens began molting. To continue to lay eggs, they would need a light in the chicken house. Chickens need 14 hours of daylight to lay eggs on a consistent basis.

In that our family is fairly large, we needed more eggs than what our 6 hens were providing. We bought 12 more chicks and worked up to 50! They have been great for our garden as they search for insects. We do have to keep an eye on them or they will eat our produce. They love figs! Scott and the boys built a great little chicken coop and the boys all take turns tending to them. We still continue to use the chicken tractor for new chicks that are ready to roam, but not ready to be with the adult chickens. If the chicks are introduced to the adult hens too early, the hens will peck the poor chicks to death.

Raising chickens has been one of the most rewarding and beneficial decisions our family has made. Chickens supply us with one of the most versatile forms of protein on a self-sustaining farm whether you raise the birds just for the eggs, or both the meat and eggs. Nothing goes into the chickens that you do not give them. There are no antibiotics, genetically modified meats, or growth hormones in them. They are easy to care for and the harvest is no less than fabulous!

Because our chickens are fed scraps from the table and are given freedom to run around in the yard, they are healthier birds, therefore giving us healthier meat and eggs. Both the meat and eggs are higher in Omega-3 fatty acid, contain less cholesterol

A chicken tractor is a moveable low to the ground chicken coop. It allows the chicken to eat and scratch in different parts of the yard as you move the tractor. It aerates the ground as well as provides nutrients to the chickens.

and saturated fat and more vitamins and folic acid than those of caged birds. The yolks of the eggs are richer in color. Those of you who eat the meat from the old laying hens and roosters will find that the meat is more succulent and flavorful.

Some of you will decide never to dine on your beloved chickens, but if you ever have the chance to eat a meal prepared with an old Rooster or laying hen, your taste buds will be enlightened and you will forever crave this heavenly delight! Roosters and aging hens need quite different treatment than your average roaster or broiler.

As these chickens roam free and scratch for insects, they gain muscle and connective tissue, which produce incredible body in stews, dumplings, and broth because it melts into collagen as you braise it. The flavor of the broth and the chicken is exceptional and cannot be matched.

There are three major components to achieve tender domestic poultry.

1. Domestic free-range organic laying hens or roosters must be refrigerated or aged for at least 3 days. (I age it for 5 days and keep it on a rack not allowing it to sit in any blood).
2. Braise it on low heat for at least 3 to 5 hours.
3. After braising, allow it to rest in the refrigerator overnight if time permits.

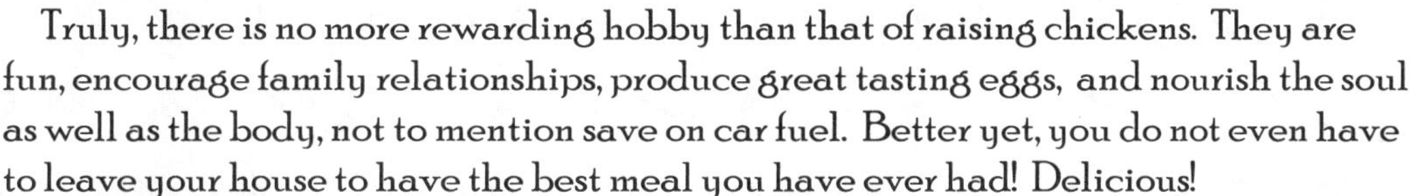

Truly, there is no more rewarding hobby than that of raising chickens. They are fun, encourage family relationships, produce great tasting eggs, and nourish the soul as well as the body, not to mention save on car fuel. Better yet, you do not even have to leave your house to have the best meal you have ever had! Delicious!

The most consistent laying hens are Buff Orpingtons, Rhode Island Reds, Dominiques, and Ameraucanas. These hens lay large eggs and the Ameraucanas will give you a beautiful light blue/green egg.

Feed your chickens from the table and give them lots of love and you will have happy chickens that lay "golden eggs"!

Avoid washing eggs to protect the bloom. The bloom is the protective coating on the outside of the shell. If you must wash them, eat them with in a few days in that they will not last as long as those that have not been washed. Some people recommend putting hand sanitizer on the outside to kill any bacteria right before cracking the egg.

If you notice your eggshells are soft, bake eggshells in a 350 degree oven for 5 minutes, crush, and feed them to your chickens. This will give them extra calcium in their diets.

If you are using an organic chicken as opposed to a rooster or old hen, you may only need to simmer chicken for one hour.

To reheat, sprinkle a little water into your microwavable bowl and microwave until hot. Stop every minute or so and stir as gently as possible.

Tim's Hint: If it's too dry, add a little buttermilk; too wet, dust with flour and continue to knead. It's ok to overwork dumpling dough.

Big Mama's Southern Chicken *and* Buttermilk Dumplings

Serves 8–10

One of my favorite "foodie" friends, Tim Martin, shared his "Chicken and Dunklin" recipe that just had to make it in this book. After I made it for the fourth time, I thought to myself, "Why is it that I love this recipe so much?" I was stumped, and then I made it again when it came to me that every time I ate this recipe, thoughts of my grandmother cooking over her stove popped into my head. When she served Chicken and Dumplings, she talked incessantly of her mama, "Big Mama," teaching her how to make them. I think those are her favorite memories.

The best tasting chickens are those that have been free to roam and are slow-grown working their muscles as they find insects for food. Especially in these low and slow recipes, the flavor is absolutely more luscious and silky than those that are young chickens.

Stock Ingredients

1 whole free range organic chicken
4 quarts (1 gallon) water
3 stalks celery, chopped
2 carrots
1 Vidalia or yellow onion, chopped
5 sprigs parsley
5 sprigs rosemary
3 whole garlic cloves
1 stick unsalted butter
1tablespoon Kosher salt
½ tablespoon pepper

Dumplings

3 cups self-rising flour
½ cup shortening
2 teaspoons Kosher salt
½ cup buttermilk,
plus more if dough is too dry

Bring chicken, water, celery, carrots, onion, parsley, rosemary, garlic, and butter to a boil, reduce heat and simmer uncovered for at least 3 hours or until the chicken falls off the bones. Make sure to skim the foam as needed.

Meanwhile, in a large mixing bowl, combine flour and salt. Cut shortening into flour until fully incorporated. Add buttermilk slowly into the flour a little at the time. When the dough is easily formed into a ball, knead the dough.

Roll out the dough to a thickness of 1⁄16 of an inch or even thinner. Pinch or cut into 1 inch squares (I use a pizza cutter for this). Set aside.

When chicken is falling off the bone, remove the pieces to a plate. Strain the broth throwing away vegetables and herbs.

Add broth back to the pot and add butter, salt and pepper. Bring to a boil and lower to a simmer. Pull all the meat from the chicken and shred. Return chicken to the broth.

Add the dumplings to the broth and bring to a hard boil. Allow them to boil about 2 minutes and turn off the heat. Stir gently with a wooden spoon every few minutes for the next 30 minutes. This step releases the starch in the dumplings, promotes creaminess, and intensifies the buttery flavors!

Chicken Farmer's Style

Serves 4

This dish really is one of my favorite preparations of old chickens. This is one of the first recipes I created from my study of historic techniques used in France to cook their old laying hens. I have updated some of the ingredients but the technique is the same.

Brine Ingredients

1 cup Kosher salt
½ cup brown sugar
1 tablespoon peppercorns
2 scallions, chopped
2 cloves of garlic
¼ teaspoon allspice
1 quart chicken stock
2 quarts water

Ingredients

1 chicken, quartered and rinsed
Freshly ground black pepper
12 slices pancetta
2 tablespoons butter
2 tablespoons extra virgin olive oil
4 large carrots, cut into 1 inch lengths
3 cloves garlic, thinly sliced
1 onion, diced to ¼ inch
3 bay leaves
3 sprigs rosemary
3 stalk celery
1 cup dry white wine
1 pound whole Homemade Canned Tomatoes
Or 15 oz. canned tomatoes
¼ cup Italian parsley, finely chopped

Combine Kosher salt, brown sugar, peppercorns, scallions, garlic, and allspice in a saucepan. Add chicken stock and bring to a boil stirring to dissolve the salt and sugar. Remove from heat and allow to cool.

Combine the cooled mixture with remaining water in pot big enough to hold the chicken and stir well. Add quartered chicken and refrigerate overnight.

Remove chicken from brine and pat dry with towels. Season with pepper.

Wrap each piece of quartered chicken in a slice of pancetta and secure with a toothpick. In skillet heat olive oil and butter over high heat. Add chicken and brown for about 10 minutes on each side. Do not crowd or they will not brown. Transfer to plate.

Add carrots, garlic, onion, bay leaves, rosemary, and celery to pan and cook about 5 minutes. Add the wine and tomatoes. Crush the tomatoes as you place them in the pot. Add chicken and reduce heat to simmer. Cook uncovered for about 30 minutes or until chicken is no longer pink. Transfer chicken to a serving platter.

Adjust seasoning. Add parsley. Pour sauce over meat. Serve with Garlic Mashed Potatoes.

This recipe is great using pheasant.

Chicken *and* Mushrooms *over* Cheesy Grits

Comfort. That is what this meal represents. The garlic and tender chicken mixed with creamy, salty, cheesy grits with a gravy-like sauce with mushrooms...comfort... scrumptious...amazing!

Do not add cheese until right before serving. The cheese will separate and become grainy.

Use any mushrooms available, but for best flavor use a variety of mushrooms. Just remember to keep the total amount of mushrooms the same as the recipe.

Ingredients

4 chicken thighs, skin removed and deboned
½ teaspoon kosher salt
¼ teaspoon freshly ground pepper
¼ cup all purpose flour
1 tablespoon olive oil
2 large onions, cut into 1 inch pieces
3 garlic cloves, minced
2 large carrots, cut into 1 inch pieces
8 ounces of Baby Bella mushrooms, halved
4 ounces button mushrooms, halved
4 ounces Shitake mushrooms, stemmed and sliced
1 tablespoon rosemary, chopped
1½ cups chicken broth

In a shallow dish, combine flour, salt, and pepper and coat the chicken in mixture. Reserve 1 tablespoon leftover flour. Place the oil in a large pot and heat over medium-high heat. When oil is shimmering, add the chicken and cook for 5-7 minutes or until brown on all sides. Remove to a plate.

Reduce the heat to medium, stir the onions into the pot, and cook for 2 minutes. Add garlic and cook for 30 seconds. Whisk in the reserved 1 tablespoon of flour and cook for 1 minute. Stir in chicken broth, carrots, mushrooms, and rosemary and place the chicken into the vegetables and bring to a boil. Partly cover and simmer over medium-low heat for 25-30 minutes, or until the chicken is no longer pink in the middle and the vegetables are tender. Plate warm, atop a scoop of cheese grits.

Cheesy Grits

Ingredients

5 cups water or chicken stock
1 cup grits
3 tablespoons butter
½ teaspoon salt
½ teaspoon pepper
½ cup Parmesan-Reggiano

Add grits, butter, salt, and pepper to the water or stock. Bring to a boil stirring constantly, and then reduce to simmer for about 30 minutes, stirring occasionally.

Just before serving, add the Parmesan and stir until dissolved.

Healthy Chicken Soup

Serves 4

I can't help but feel warm and fuzzy every time my mom serves me Chicken Soup. I think she was a firm believer that chicken soup had medicinal properties. Who can argue with that?

Homemade chicken stock

Ingredients

3 5 pound whole free range roasting chickens
3 large yellow onions, unpeeled, quartered
6 carrots, unpeeled and halved
4 celery stalks with leaves, cut in thirds
20 sprigs fresh parsley
15 sprigs fresh thyme
20 sprigs fresh dill
1 head garlic, unpeeled, cut in half crosswise
2 tablespoons Kosher salt
2 teaspoons whole black peppercorns

To make the stock

Cut chickens into several pieces. Place chicken, onions, carrots, celery stalks, parsley, thyme, dill, garlic, salt, and pepper in a large stockpot. Add 7 quarts of water. Bring to a boil and simmer for 6 hours. Turn burner off and let it sit for 1 hour. Strain. Pull the chicken off of the bone and reserve for another use.

Place chicken stock in refrigerator overnight. The next day, remove the surface fat. Use immediately or freeze for up to 3 months.

Old hens and roosters have always been preferred over broiler chickens for making chicken soup because of their rich flavor in the chicken broth. Chinese 5 spice, a blend of star anise, clover, fennel seed, cinnamon and Sichuan pepper, can be eliminated from this recipe, but I personally think it adds a special touch to the dish.

Stock has higher bone content than broth which produces a better base for sauces and soups.

Ingredients for soup

2 tablespoons olive oil
2 Vidalia onions, chopped
1 clove garlic, minced
4 cups celery, chopped

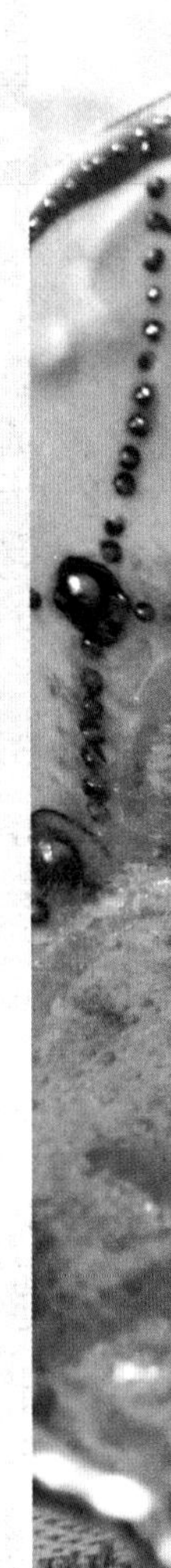

3 cups carrots, chopped
¾ cup Italian parsley, chopped and divided
2 tablespoons rosemary, chopped
¼ teaspoon Chinese 5 spice
4 pounds and 4 cups chicken meat, shredded
1 quart chicken stock
1 tablespoon Kosher salt
½ teaspoon freshly ground pepper

In a large crock heat olive oil until simmering. Add onions and sauté until onions are translucent. Add garlic and sauté for 30 seconds more.

Add celery, carrots, ½ cup parsley, rosemary, Chinese 5 Spice, salt and pepper, chicken, and stock. Stir ingredients well.

Bring mixture to a boil then reduce heat and let simmer for 1 hour stirring occasionally. Ladle into bowls and serve with remaining parsley.

Just a Note about Wild Turkey

Wild turkeys are built for survival. They easily fly and are very fast runners building up quite a lot of muscle and connective tissue. The diet of domestic turkeys is that mostly of corn and grain while wild turkeys feast on a diverse diet consisting of berries, herbs, grass, and insects. Domestic Turkeys cannot fly or run fast. They are bred to have very large breasts and this causes them to be quite unstable and unable to exercise. The wild turkeys that the boys bring home are much older than the domestic variety.

Because of all these differences, the size, flavor, and texture of the turkey is greatly affected. Wild turkey will have much more depth of flavor, but if not prepared correctly will be tough. There are many injector kits available to add moisture to the meat if you are frying or roasting the turkey, but my favorite application of cooking wild turkey is to quarter, brown, and braise the pieces. I also love stuffing the breast as well as slicing, pounding, and frying the cutlets. All of these methods break down the connective tissue and muscle fiber making it so tender that you can easily cut it with a fork. The stock that a turkey carcass provides is excellent as well. There is not much better eating than the wild turkey, a traditional American favorite.

All of my recipes are adaptable between domesticated turkeys and wild turkeys.

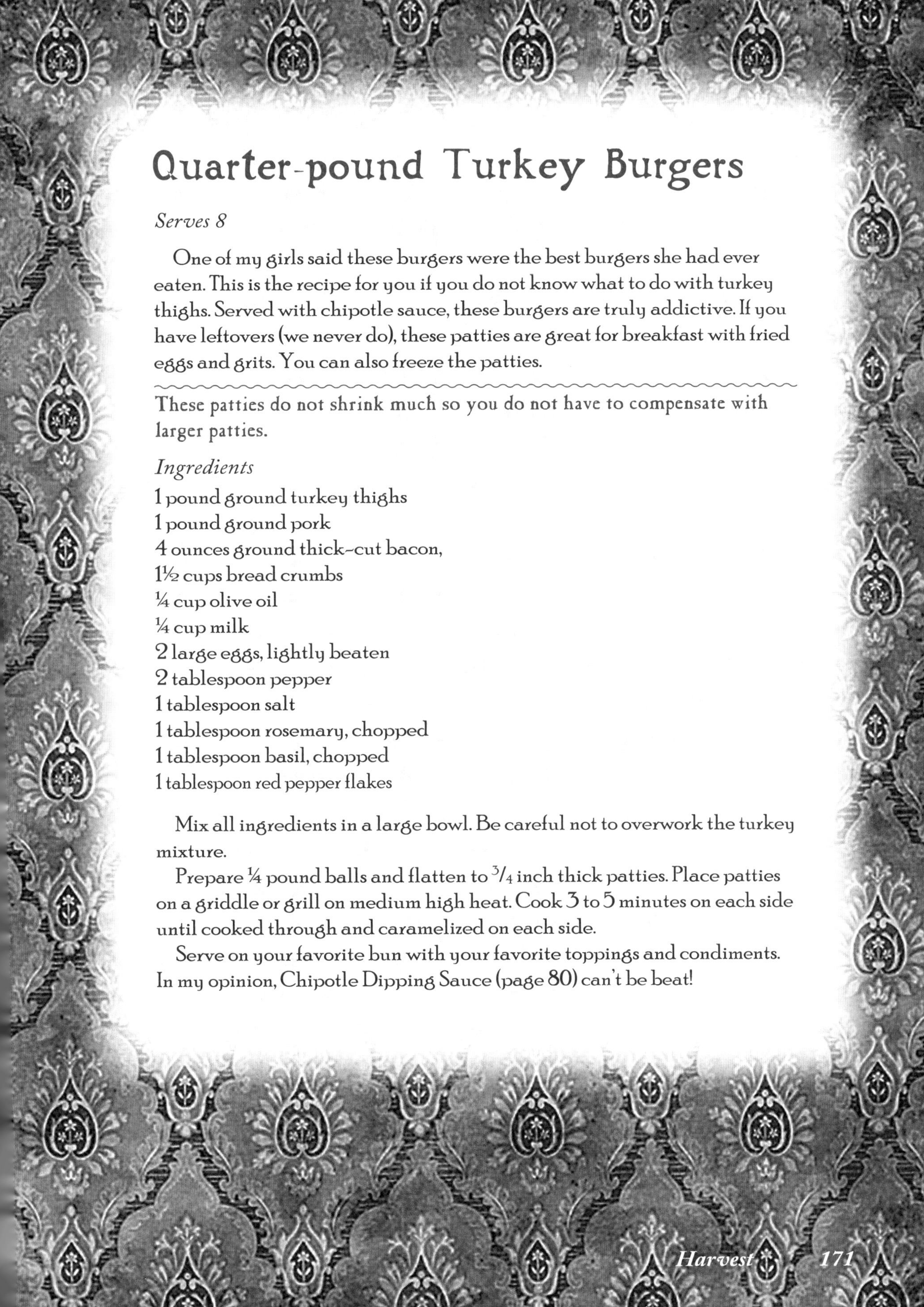

Quarter-pound Turkey Burgers

Serves 8

One of my girls said these burgers were the best burgers she had ever eaten. This is the recipe for you if you do not know what to do with turkey thighs. Served with chipotle sauce, these burgers are truly addictive. If you have leftovers (we never do), these patties are great for breakfast with fried eggs and grits. You can also freeze the patties.

These patties do not shrink much so you do not have to compensate with larger patties.

Ingredients

1 pound ground turkey thighs
1 pound ground pork
4 ounces ground thick-cut bacon,
1½ cups bread crumbs
¼ cup olive oil
¼ cup milk
2 large eggs, lightly beaten
2 tablespoon pepper
1 tablespoon salt
1 tablespoon rosemary, chopped
1 tablespoon basil, chopped
1 tablespoon red pepper flakes

Mix all ingredients in a large bowl. Be careful not to overwork the turkey mixture.

Prepare ¼ pound balls and flatten to ¾ inch thick patties. Place patties on a griddle or grill on medium high heat. Cook 3 to 5 minutes on each side until cooked through and caramelized on each side.

Serve on your favorite bun with your favorite toppings and condiments. In my opinion, Chipotle Dipping Sauce (page 80) can't be beat!

Asian Skewered Turkey *with* Chili Ginger Dipping Sauce

Serves 10

I served these winning turkey skewers at a wedding party that I gave to my adorable niece. Turkey skewers are great for any occasion from weddings to tailgate parties!

Add snow peas to the mix and serve over rice noodles with a few splashes of low sodium soy sauce and make this dish into a meal.

Asian skewered turkey with chili ginger sauce

Asian Turkey Ingredients

2 tablespoons dark sesame seed oil
2 tablespoons rice wine vinegar
1.5 tablespoons garlic, minced
1 tablespoon soy sauce
1 skinless boneless turkey breast

Chili Ginger Dip

1½ tablespoons fresh ginger root, minced
2 tablespoons soy sauce
1 tablespoon rice wine vinegar
3 tablespoons lemon juice
1 teaspoon sesame oil
2 tablespoons chili paste
½ cup mayonnaise
Tabasco to taste

Cut turkey breast into 1-inch wide slices against the grain of the meat. Pound slices into ¼ inch thickness, then cut pounded pieces into about 1½ inch by 5 inch strips.

In a large bowl mix the dark sesame seed oil, rice wine vinegar, garlic, and soy sauce and pour over the turkey. Massage gently into meat. Cover and refrigerate overnight.

Thread each piece of marinated turkey onto skewers. Heat griddle or grill until almost smoking. Cook turkey for about 3 minutes, turn over and cook for 2 more minutes.

In a medium sized bowl combine ginger, soy sauce, rice wine vinegar, lemon juice, sesame oil, chili paste, mayonnaise, and Tabasco. Mix well. Place dip in a serving bowl. Arrange with the skewers and have fun!

Stuffed Turkey Breast

Serves 4 to 6

If you ask me, you just can't beat Stuffed Turkey. This dish not only has a beautiful presentation, but also has the flavor punch that my family craves. The aromas of the buttery turkey and herbs will fill your house with warmth. The flavors of the stuffing and the tenderness of the turkey make for a succulent meal for any occasion. I can see this dish served on Christmas night and any day of the week!

Ingredients

¼ cup mushrooms, sautéed and chopped
½ cup Parmesan cheese, grated
½ cup artichoke hearts
¼ cup parsley, chopped
2 garlic cloves, minced
1 teaspoon kosher salt
½ teaspoon freshly ground pepper
1 1 pound turkey breast

Preheat oven to 350 degrees.

Place mushrooms, cheese, artichokes, parsley, garlic, salt, and pepper in a food processor and pulse until blended.

Butterfly turkey breast as shown on page 240. Pound turkey breast to ¼ inch thick. You should end up with about a 10x6 rectangle.

Place artichoke mixture on center of pounded turkey leaving an inch border around the edges. With long side facing you, roll away from you into medium tight cylinder. Truss turkey breast as shown on page 241.

Coat turkey in olive oil. Generously salt and pepper turkey. Place turkey on smoking hot skillet and brown on all sides. Place turkey in oven and bake for about 30 minutes or until turkey registers 140 degrees.

Transfer turkey to cutting board and allow to rest for 5–10 minutes. Remove twine and slice with ½ inch slices and serve.

Turkey Cutlets *with* Mixed Greens *and* Herb Vinaigrette

Serves 4

There is nothing as flavorful as organic turkey with herb vinaigrette. The tanginess of the Balsamic Vinegar and earthiness of the herbs paired with the buttery, tender, goodness of the turkey just melts in your mouth and leaves you craving more. This is one dish that is deliciously unforgettable!

This dish is nice with shaved Parmesan as well.

Ingredients

1 turkey breast
1 cup flour
1 tablespoon salt
½ tablespoon pepper
2 eggs
1 tablespoon water
1 cup bread crumbs
4 tablespoons Olive oil for frying (divided)
4 tablespoons butter (divided)
4 cups mixed greens
1 cup Herb Vinaigrette, (page 110)
2 tablespoons fresh parsley, chopped

Cut turkey breast into ¾ inch pieces. Pound to ¼ inch thick with a meat mallet.

On a large plate mix flour, salt, and pepper. On a second plate beat eggs and water together. On a third plate place breadcrumbs. Dredge dry pounded turkey breast pieces into seasoned flour mix, then egg mixture, then breadcrumbs.

In a hot sauté pan, melt butter and oil. When sizzling, place turkey in pan and brown for about 2 minutes per side. Cook in batches. Do not crowd the pan. Transfer to a platter and keep warm.

In a medium sized bowl mix greens with ¼ cup vinaigrette. Divide salad among 4 plates. Place a piece of fried turkey on top of greens. Garnish with fresh parsley and drizzle extra vinaigrette as desired (page 110).

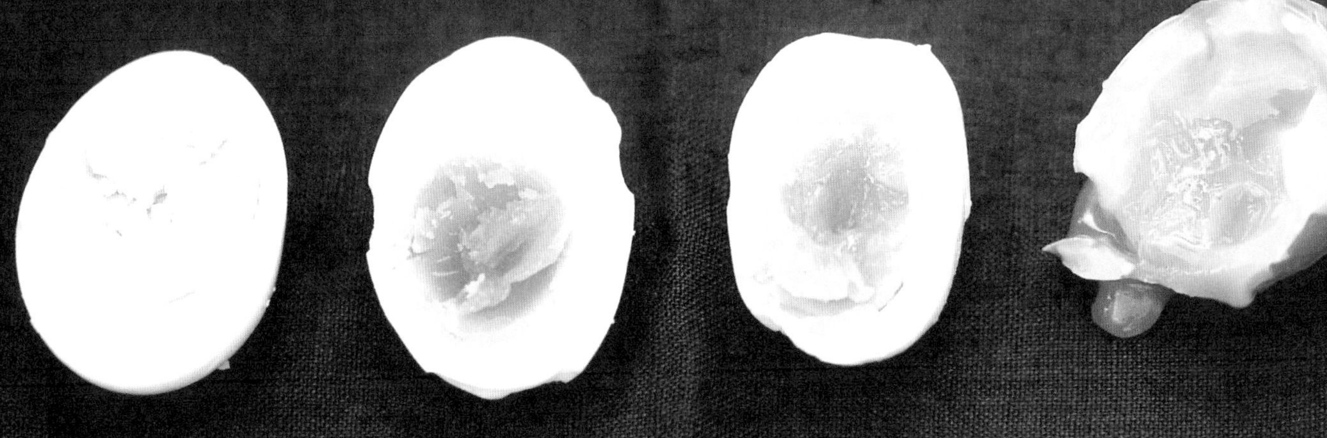

The Perfect Boiled Egg

I have been eating boiled eggs almost every week since birth, but for most of my life I guessed at the length of time to cook them. I determined to find a foolproof method of cooking the perfect boiled egg and I think I have found it.

I have tried starting the eggs in hot water, starting with cold water, keeping the water at simmer after reaching a boil, turning stovetop completely off, etc. Finally, I found the foolproof way to boil an egg. You may have to vary the times a little to get "your" perfect egg.

Place the eggs in a medium saucepan and cover eggs about an inch with cool water.

Add 1 tablespoon of salt to the water. This helps the protein in the whites, if they should crack, to quickly coagulate.

Bring the water to a rolling boil by setting the pan over high heat, uncovered.

Turn off the heat and cover the pan. Set your timer to the times below for preferred egg doneness.

- 3 minutes — soft boiled egg
- 4 minutes — soft yolk hard boiled egg
- 6 minutes — hard boiled egg
- 9 minutes — firm yolk hard boiled egg

Thoroughly tap and crack eggs on kitchen counter gently, then peel shell starting from the fat side of the egg. If you are cooking very soft boiled, skip this step.

Place the eggs in a bowl filled with ice water for a minute or two.

Peel, slice, and eat!

Older eggs have larger air cells, therefore they float in water. Older eggs are better for peeling, but new eggs are better for baking and poaching.

Southern Style Eggs Benedict with Hollandaise Sauce

Serves 4

This scrumptious dish is a perfect brunch on a warm sunny day. With it's laid back quality, it would be welcome for a casual or a celebratory meal.

Ingredients

12 fresh asparagus spears, trimmed
Kosher salt and freshly ground pepper
8 slices of no-nitrate bacon
4 biscuits cut in half (page 121)
4 eggs
Hollandaise sauce (page 181)

Use frozen biscuits to cut down on cooking time.

Preheat oven to 425 degrees. Place asparagus on cookie sheet. Drizzle with olive oil and season with salt and pepper. Bake for about 5 minutes or until asparagus is tender.

Meanwhile, in a large sauté pan over medium high heat fry 8 slices of bacon. Remove bacon to a paper towel and draw all but about 1 tablespoon of bacon drippings.

Prepare hollandaise sauce and set aside.

Reheat bacon renderings on medium heat. Slowly and carefully crack eggs into sauté pan with the bacon drippings. Cook over medium until whites are almost opaque. Put lid on sauté pan. Cook until whites are opaque. Season with a pinch of salt and pepper.

While eggs cook, divide sliced biscuits among 4 plates. Place 2 bacon slices across the sliced biscuits, then layer asparagus, Hollandaise sauce and then top with egg. Serve immediately.

Hollandaise Sauce

Yields 1 cup

Hollandaise sauce is an absolute must for Eggs Benedict. It can be quite finicky and is difficult to reheat, but I think very worthwhile to make. The benefits of this sauce far out way the costs. Once you master the sauce the applications for its use are endless.

Serve Hollandaise sauce over fish, steaks, chicken, and vegetables.

Ingredients

4 egg yolks
1 tablespoon lemon juice
1 tablespoon water
½ cup unsalted butter (1 stick), room temperature
Pinch of salt
Pinch cayenne pepper

If sauce is too thick add a little more lemon juice.

In a medium-sized sauce pan, whisk together egg yolks, water, and lemon juice until thick and light yellow. Over low heat, continue mixing fairly quickly. Try not to let the egg yolks cook too fast. You may have to remove it from the heat source every once in a while. The eggs should become frothy and double in volume.

Once mixture has doubled in volume and the eggs are smooth add a tablespoon of soft butter. Whisk continually to emulsify.

Add another tablespoon of butter and so on until the sauce has thickened to the consistency you desire. You may not need to use all of the butter.

Season with salt and cayenne pepper. Taste and adjust the seasoning. Serve lukewarm.

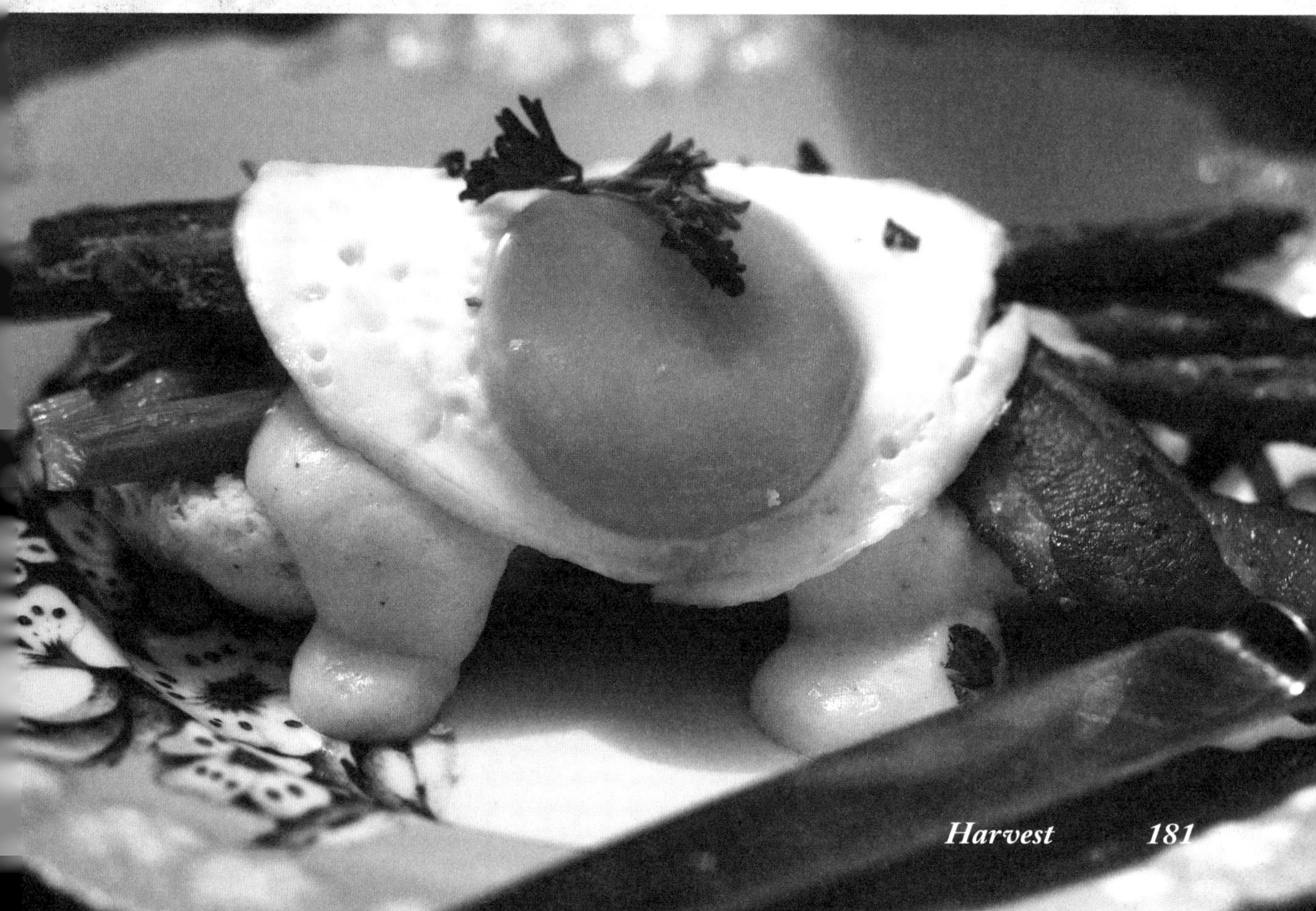

Egg Salad Sandwiches

Serves 10

Egg salad sandwiches always remind me of family reunions and picnics. It's easy to make and it's a great make-ahead meal. I like to make a double batch; one for Sunday brunch with a tomato salad and the leftovers for the next day… Monday! I always need an easy lunch and dinner for Mondays.

If you are not eating these immediately, store them in wax paper in the refrigerator. They will last for about 3 hours.

Ingredients

12 hard boiled eggs, peeled
½ onion, diced
1 cup celery, diced
1 cup pickles, diced
½ cup mayonnaise (preferably homemade)
1 tablespoon whole grain mustard
½ teaspoon pepper
Sourdough bread, sliced
½ cup mixed lettuce

In a large bowl, smash the eggs with a fork until the whites of the eggs look diced. Stir in the onion, celery, pickles, mayonnaise, mustard, and pepper.

Divide egg salad among half the slices of bread. Add the lettuce next atop the egg salad. Top with remaining slices of bread.

Homemade Mayonnaise

Yields approximately 1 pint

It seems every time I need mayonnaise, I cannot find a drop in the house. Instead of going to the grocery store I began making a recipe that I was given for homemade mayonnaise and surprisingly it only took five minutes and it tasted so fresh, bright and just plain GREAT.

Ingredients

1 egg
2 egg yolks
1 teaspoon Dijon mustard
1½ tablespoons Meyer lemon juice
½ 1teaspoon salt
¼ teaspoon white pepper
2 cups olive oil

In a food processor add egg, egg yolks, lemon juice, mustard, salt, and white pepper.

Start food processor and run continuously while very slowly adding drops of oil waiting 30 seconds between each drop. Continue with the drops for about ¼ cup of oil.

When mayonnaise has definitely thickened add oil in a stream. You may not need all the oil at this time therefore check after each ½ cup is added for thickness and taste. If the consistency of mayonnaise is very thick, add a drop of lemon to thin it or if too thin add more oil.

Place mayonnaise in a bowl and serve or keep covered in refrigerator for one week.

Never use aluminum bowls or saucepans to prepare mayonnaise, as they will turn the mayonnaise gray. Also store it in plastic, glass, or stainless steel as well.

Use the freshest available eggs possible.

All ingredients must be at room temperature.

From the Pasture

Beef, It's What's for Dinner

With so many label options on beef at the market, one is likely to throw their hands up and buy chicken. Well, that brings a new set of labels on their own...maybe just become a vegetarian.

In this article, I hope to dispel any confusion swirling around in your head about the labels on packages of beef making your shopping a little more joyful.

Before the 1950's, cattle farming looked consistently the same as hundreds of years before. Farmers used no antibiotics, no hormones, and always finished them off with grass, because feedlots did not largely exist. Testing in the 50's proved utilizing hormones (which, incidentally, were unprofitable for swine, poultry, and goats and thereby, quickly outlawed) and feedlots proved more economically sound, allowing faster muscle mass and shorter turnaround.

With all the new and improved technical advances, we as consumers must ask several questions – What shall we consume? Do these added changes really matter? What will bring the best and highest nutritional value to our families? How far should all of this super technology go when dealing with what fuels our bodies?

Dispelling the goods on BEEF LABELS

No added hormones- Just that.

There are several different types of hormones. A couple of major hormones are hormonal growth implants and beta-adrenergic agonist, known as growth promoters. Many cattle get treated with hormonal growth implants, a small pellet injected on back of ear slowly feeding gonadotropins (natural or synthetic sex hormones) to the cow, which encouraging more muscle growth and less fat. As of late, many feedlots have begun to use beta-adrenergic agonist as part of the finishing regimen. This drug basically creates a suspended adrenaline-like state, keeping nutrients more in the muscles and less in the guts, allowing better body mass: muscle ratio.

No antibiotics - Same principle as human antibiotics.

Most farmers use antibiotics to heal or prevent disease in cattle. They are often used at the farm like we use them, to stop an infection. Cattle usually get a preventative dose of antibiotics as they come into the feedlots.

Another type of antibiotic, ionophores, works a little different. Ionophores, again, a type of growth promoter like the hormones, act in the rumen to correct the bacteria balance offset by the acid pH of the limited diet of corn in many (but by far not all) feedlots. (Also, read the words carefully. For instance, "No antibiotics" is not the same as "no antibiotic residues," the latter does not mean that the cattle never had antibiotics, but, in accordance with law, waited the determined amount of days to allow the antibiotic to work out (or nearly so) before slaughter.)

Organic–

The USDA considers livestock "organic" and puts their seal on the meat when, "...Producers met animal health and welfare standards, did not use antibiotics or growth hormones, used 100% organic feed, and provided animals with access to the outdoors."

The USDA adds a little challenge to all tiers of raising cattle. Organically grown cattle live in good conditions complete with outdoor space to exercise and breathe fresh air, clean water to drink, and shelter from the elements. Most cattle receive humane treatment at the farm, but organic regulations assure good treatment at the feedlots. Like most other cattle farming methods, pasture and forage consist of at least part of the cattle's diet. While some organic cattle feed purely on grass, further earning the grass-fed standard (below), the remaining (perhaps the majority) of the diet consists of organically produced feed (hay, soy, corn, etc.). Note that because the corn and other grains fed to the cattle are organic, they contain no GMOs.

Farmers have much higher expenses when producing organic cattle. Without hormones, cattle grow much slower, hence SLOW FOOD, increasing the time on the farm. Organic feed costs more than traditional feed, and without hormones to increase the cattle's growing rate, quickly raises the farmer's overhead. Therefore, if you wish to buy organic, be prepared to pay premiums. The Organic Beef Profile reported that organic beef cost 45% more than grain-fed beef in the beginning of 2011.

Grass (forage) fed– Fed on grass, not grain, throughout life.

Grass-fed cattle must have continuous access to pasture during growing season. Grass-fed cattle may or may not be organic. By this method, farmers have the option to treat their stock with hormones and antibiotics. However, farmers generally use less drugs since these cattle skip the feedlots.

According to a 2010 review by Nutrition Journal, grass-fed beef possesses more nutritional value than grain-fed contemporaries. The study showed grass-fed beef to not only contain less fat, but the existing fat to have a better ratio of saturated fatty acids than grain fed beef, better for cholesterol. The study found grass-fed beef contains more good fatty acids like conjugated linoleic acid, trans-vaccenic acid, and omega-3 fatty acids. Also contains higher levels of vitamin A and E precursors and cancer fighting antioxidants.

As a side note to taste, grass-fed beef has a distinctive taste. Because of this, many people prefer grain-fed beef. The University of Georgia performed a study on the market for "grass-finished" beef, or beef from cattle not finished at the feedlot, in the Southeast. Their participants preferred (by a small margin, none the less) grain-fed to grass-fed beef. Another study found similar results in the North. The study done by Nutrition Journal argues many Americans prefer corn-fed beef because of familiarity. People preferred what they grew up eating.

Though the taste tests do contain interesting information and results, I believe the tests had a significant error; the cooking preparation –namely, temperature pertaining to doneness. Like previously stated, grass fed beef contains less fat (i.e., marbling) than grain fed beef. Because of this, the former must be treated a little different from the latter. Grass fed beef, like venison, quickly become dry and tough cooked beyond 150° or to "medium." Grain-fed beef have more fat, allowing a little more forgiveness to the cook. Both aforementioned tests cooked the meat to around 160°, or in other words, "well done."

I give much credence to the theory of preference from familiarity. Grass-fed beef, or organic beef, does present a different flavor than their grain-fed counterparts. ...I think grass-fed beef, however, has flavor, corn-finished tasting bland in comparison.

In conclusion there are a few more terms that need addressing.

Natural-

A much more ambiguous term simply means minimally processed and contain no artificial ingredients or synthetic ingredients (food coloring, preservative, etc.). Pertains purely to processing. Some, but not all, accomplish the "natural" label by adding no hormones or antibiotics to the cattle and finishing them off in pastures rather than feedlots. Personally, I would not pay more for this beef because of the ambiguity of the regulations.

Free-range – provided continuous access to food and water, in a structure, and an outdoor environment.

Cage-free – Allowed to mingle and have unlimited access to food and water.

Pasture raised – Not standardized.

Humane - Not standardized.

Although very confusing, these labels are worth decoding.

In some foods, I do not think that it is as important to eat "organic" as others, but concerning the meat that I put in my body, "organic" is the best choice for me and my family. Although extremely expensive, the value outweighs the hardship. I agree that many more studies need to be conducted as to the effect of added hormones and antibiotics in beef have on the human body, but until then I will remain as "pure" in my meat choice as possible.

One of my favorite cuts of meat...beef short ribs. Oh my goodness, they are scrumptious. I think they have antidepressant effects. Just try it. Feed them to anyone feeling blue and you watch the healing transformation take place!

Braised Short Ribs and Ginger Gremolata

Serves 4

Ingredients

¼ cup extra-virgin olive oil
4 16-ounce beef short ribs
Kosher salt and freshly ground pepper
1 onion, peeled and roughly chopped
3 carrots, peeled and roughly chopped
3 celery stalks, roughly chopped
6 garlic cloves (2 Tablespoons), minced
2 cups full-bodied red wine
1 16 ounce can of tomatoes with the juices
2 cups beef stock
½ bunch of thyme (about ¼ cup), roughly chopped
½ bunch of rosemary (about ¼ cup), roughly chopped
½ bunch of oregano (about ¼ cup)

Gremolata

Ingredients

Leaves from 1 ½ bunch of flat-leaf parsley
Zest of 1 lemon
Zest of 1 orange
¼ pound fresh ginger, minced

Preheat the oven to 350 degrees.

In a large heavy bottom Dutch oven, heat oil until almost smoking. Liberally season the ribs with the salt and pepper and brown the ribs over high heat on all sides until the meat is deep brown, about 15-20 minutes. Don't skip this step or the flavor will not be as intense. Remove the short ribs to a plate and set aside.

Add the onions, carrots, and celery to the Dutch oven until they are translucent, about 10 minutes. Add the garlic for about 2 minutes then stir in the red wine, tomatoes with the juice, beef stock, thyme, rosemary, and oregano. Scrape the bottom of the pan with a wooden spoon to remove the browned bits. Cover and place in the oven for 2 hours or until the meat is falling off the bone.

To make the gremolata: In a small bowl, lightly toss the parsley, lemon zest, orange zest, and fresh ginger.

Remove the short ribs from the oven and remove to a plate. Pour the pan juices over the ribs and place a handful of gremolata over the top of them, and serve with Garlic Mashed Potatoes.

Growing up, my family's Thursday nights staple was pork chops on the grill. My step-dad liked well done, thin pork chops. To say the least, they weren't my favorite... I never knew that pork chops could be any different until Scott made them for me one night. They were perfectly juicy and tender; nothing like I had ever experienced. I found my new favorite food that night.

Pork chops don't have a lot of fat and are prone to overcooking and drying out. That's where the cooking method of frying on top of the stove and then finishing the chops off in the oven comes in. Pork Chops tend to dry out and burn when you cook them on the stovetop alone, but by frying one side first and getting it good and brown, turning it over and putting it in the oven to finish cooking gives you the best of both worlds. The outside caramelizes, and the inside cooks slowly in the oven without burning the outside of the chop.

The brine will season the meat perfectly without the meat becoming overly salty. A brine adds flavor and keeps the meat tender and juicy. I assure you brining is worth the wait!!

One Pan Tender and Juicy Pork Chops

Serves 4

BRINE

3 cups cold water
¼ cup kosher salt
¼ cup brown sugar
2 cloves of garlic, smashed

PORK CHOPS

4 1-inch thick pork chops (4 pounds)
olive oil, for pan frying
Kosher salt
freshly ground pepper

In a saucepan combine 1 cup of water, the salt, and brown sugar bring to a simmer. Turn the heat off and stir the brine liquid until all the ingredients have dissolved in the water. Add the remaining water and garlic to the pot. Place the pork chops in a shallow dish and slowly pour the brine over the chops making sure they are submerged in the brining liquid. If the aren't submerged, add another cup of water and tablespoon of salt to the brine. Cover and refrigerate for 1 hour or up to 6 hours for thicker chops.

Preheat the oven to 400 degrees and place a cast iron skillet in the oven to preheat as well. Remove the pork chops from the brine and dry thoroughly with a paper towel. Liberally sprinkle salt and pepper on both sides of the pork chops and rub into the chops.

Carefully remove the skillet from the oven and place over high heat. Add about 2 tablespoons of olive oil to the skillet along with the pork chops. Allow to brown for about 3 minutes. Turn the chops over and transfer them to the preheated oven. Roast the chops for about 5 minutes or until they are cooked through and the temperature of the chops reads 145 degrees at the thickest part.

Remove cooked pork chops to a plate and pour pan juices over the chops. Allow to rest for 5 minutes and serve with Garlic Mashed Potatoes, a salad, and asparagus.

Smelling pork sausage on Christmas morning upon arriving at my dad's house is one of my favorite memories. I knew that the eggs were going to be made in the same pan that Dad cooked the sausage in. He never veered from his method of cooking breakfast, his favorite meal. I could always count on this, and it really means a lot to me as I pass on the same tradition to my kids. Now, my dad comes to MY house on Christmas morning and I deliver breakfast made in his same old-fashioned perfect way.

Pork Sausage

Ingredients

6 pounds of pork shoulder or neck, run through the largest holes of a grinder
¼ cup brown sugar
3 Tablespoons Kosher Salt
1 ½ Tablespoons black pepper
1 ½ Tablespoons red pepper flakes
Natural casings
½ cup red wine
6 Tablespoons extra-virgin olive oil

In a mixing bowl, stir together the pork, salt, pepper, and red wine until well blended. Do not overwork the mixture or the meat's texture will change. Set up the sausage stuffer and place casing over the funnel feeder. Begin stuffing the sausage into the casings, twisting every 4 inches.

To cook the links, heat the oil in a 14-inch skillet over medium heat until smoking. When the oil is shimmering, place the sausage into the pan and cook for 7 to 9 minutes, until dark golden brown. Turn the sausages until they are brown all over. Continue to cook until the internal temperature reaches 160 degrees F.

Serve with sautéd onions and peppers over a bed of mashed potatoes.

Gumbo has been a Louisiana favorite for over a century. In my opinion, it's the perfect fusion food. Gumbo is a perfect mix of French, West African, and American Indian Cuisine. Each culture in Louisiana made their contributions to this dish.

Gumbos have mostly been divided into two categories, those thickened with filé and those thickened with okra. It is believed that okra is used in the summer when it is fresh and file during the winter months. I don't buy that reasoning. If you've ever been in a room with Gumbo connoisseurs, a mighty big fight will usually break out over which is the "real" version of gumbo.

Although I use okra at times in gumbo, I particularly love the way filé tastes. It has a distinctive earthy flavor and adds color to the gumbo. Oftentimes folks will just thicken with a roux, but I do both for flavor and texture.

With gumbo's popularity spreading to all of America, more variations of the dish are becoming popular. Most versions contain chicken, shrimp, and sausage, but in hunter's households you will find duck, turkey, and pheasant making their way into the gumbo.

That's where the black-eyed peas in this recipes come in. In Alabama, peas are quite proficient and plentiful. Black-eyed peas just seem to naturally come up in our dirt. They're easy to harvest, shell, freeze, and dry which make them a staple on a Southerner's table. Once you try gumbo with the black-eyed peas, you'll always think something's missing when they aren't there.

Black-Eyed Pea Gumbo

Serves 16

Ingredients

1 cup vegetable oil
3 pounds Andouille sausage, cut crosswise ½-inch thick pieces
4 pounds chicken breasts, cut in 1-inch cubes
1 cup all purpose flour
4 large onions (about 8 cups), chopped
2 red bell peppers (about 2 cups), chopped
10 stalks celery (about 4 cups), chopped
14 garlic cloves, crushed
1 Tablespoon Kosher salt
1 teaspoon cayenne pepper
6 bay leaves
1 Tablespoon dried oregano
2 pounds dried black-eyed
4 quarts chicken stock. (page 161)
4 pounds of shrimp (peeled, deveined, and shell removed)
½ cup chopped chives plus more for garnish, sliced thinly
¼ cup parsley plus more for garnish, chopped
2 ½ Tablespoons file powder, recipe on page 142
White Rice, recipe below
Hot Sauce

In a large Dutch oven or pot, heat 2 tablespoons of the vegetable oil over medium-high heat. Add the sausage and brown until cooked through, about 10 minutes. Remove the sausage to paper towels and allow to drain. Brown the chicken in batches, removing to a paper towel to drain.

Add the rest of the oil to the pot over medium-high heat . When the oil is smoking add the flour and stir constantly until mixture is dark brown, about 5 minutes. Add the onions, bell pepper, and celery and cook until the onions are translucent. Stir often for about 10 minutes. Add garlic, salt, cayenne pepper, bay leaves, oregano, sausage, chicken, and black-eyed peas then stir for 2 more minutes.

Stirring, slowly add the chicken stock until well combined. Bring the mixture to a boil then reduce the heat to medium-low and cook uncovered, stirring occasionally, for one hour. Skim off any fat that rises to the surface.

Add the shrimp, green onions, parsley, and file powder and stir until well combined. Serve over rice and garnish with the extra chopped chives and parsley. Season with Hot Sauce.

Rice Recipe

Ingredients

4 cups long-grain white rice
8 cups water
2 tablespoons unsalted butter
1 tablespoon salt
2 bay leaves

In a medium-sized saucepan, combine all the ingredients and bring to a boil over high heat. Reduce the simmer and cover for about 20 minutes. Remove the pan from the heat and allow the pan to remain covered for about 5 minutes. Uncover and fluff the rice. Remove the bay leaf and serve.

This recipe is best the day you cook it. It's fine the second day, but the black-eyed peas make the gumbo a little creamy.

Easy, amazing, and quite possibly one of my favorite comfort meals of all time are my first thoughts concerning this lamb dish. This recipe of crispy edged garlic potatoes soaking up the succulent lamb with lamb sauce and gravy has my mouth watering from the moment I put the lamb in the oven.

Sheep are absolutely gorgeous animals to me. Every year as my family assesses our projects, raising sheep is always top on the list. It's very important to me that the animals we raise have the ability to be out in the open air enjoying their lives with plenty of vegetation to graze. This is especially true for sheep in that they will quickly develop respiratory illnesses if they are confined to areas that are not well-ventilated. For us to raise them adequately, we would have to remove more trees off our land so for now, I will buy from local farmers.

Believe it or not, there are local farmers in just about every city that raise sheep. They are not as hard to find as you may think. The good news is that most sheep are raised outdoors and there are very little factory farmed sheep at this time. Most likely if you are to buy lamb, it will have been properly raised and processed.

The gravy that is naturally created from the lamb drippings and a few herbs is out of this world. Lamb meat is outrageously succulent and has an earthy mild taste that is enhanced when served with smashed potatoes.

The potatoes are so easy to prepare that it is ridiculous and the taste and texture are...well, PERFECT!

There should really be no excuse for not making this dinner this week in your home. By the way, it would be the perfect dish for company. Everything pretty much just cooks itself. Serve this with asparagus and a side salad and you are in business!

Roasted Lamb with Smashed Roasted Potatoes and Garlic

Serves 6-8

LAMB AND GRAVY INGREDIENTS

1 bunch fresh rosemary (1 ounce/5 twigs)
6 cloves garlic
olive oil
3 to 4 pound shoulder of lamb, bone in
2 onions
Kosher Salt
Freshly ground pepper
2 tablespoons flour

POTATOES AND GARLIC INGREDIENTS

2 pounds red potatoes or fingerling potatoes
¼ cup extra-virgin olive oil
12 garlic cloves, peeled
2 sprigs fresh rosemary
Kosher salt
freshly ground pepper

LAMB SAUCE INGREDIENTS

2 bunches mint (2 ounces/ ¼ cup), coarsely chopped
1 tablespoon sugar
¼ cup red wine vinegar
1 tablespoon oil

For the lamb: preheat the oven to 325 degrees F. In a pestle and mortar, grind half of the rosemary leaves, garlic, a pinch of salt and pepper with about 1 tablespoon olive oil until it forms a nice paste. Massage the paste all over the lamb. Peel and halve the onions and place in a roasting tray. Place the lamb on top of the onions. Add 1½ cups of water to the pan and cover tightly with tin foil. Cook for 3 hours. Remove the lamb from the oven. If the pan is dry, add another cup of water to the pan and cook uncovered for 1 hour more or until the meat pulls away from the bone. Don't allow the lamb to dry out. Continue adding water if the pan begins to dry out. You need pan drippings for gravy.

Remove the lamb from the oven, transfer to a platter and cover loosely with foil. Pour the pan drippings into a saucepan. Add flour and stir until well incorporated. Add 1 cup hot water to the pan and bring gravy to a boil then lower to a simmer. Allow the gravy to simmer until the gravy coats the back of a spoon. Strain gravy through a sieve into a gravy bowl.

For the Smashed Roasted Potatoes and Garlic: add potatoes to a medium pot, cover potatoes with salted water and bring to a boil over medium-high heat. Cook about 20 minutes or until fork-tender. Drain the potatoes and allow them to cool and dry. Pour potatoes onto a sheet pan lined with parchment paper. Smash each potato with the palm of your hand until they are flat.

Drizzle the potatoes with olive oil and sprinkle with salt and pepper. Distribute the garlic cloves among the potatoes and add the rosemary springs. Place the potatoes into the oven with the lamb and cook for 20 minutes or until potatoes are golden; crunchy on the outside and creamy on the inside. Remove from the oven and serve as a bed for the lamb.

For the Lamb Sauce: in a small bowl stir the mint, sugar, vinegar, and oil until well-mixed.

To plate: Place a serving of potatoes in the middle of a serving plate for a bed for the lamb. Place a few slices of lamb on top of the potatoes. Dollop a tablespoon or so of lamb sauce over the lamb and pour the gravy over the entire dish. Serve with a salad and crusty bread.

Woods and Water

Venison, The Other Red Meat

I often hear people say that venison is "tough and has a gamey taste". I have to admit that the first half of my life, I thought the same way. I had only eaten venison once at a wild game supper and it was pretty horrible to say the least. Then.... I met Scott. My life and dining habits from then on would be drastically different. He always kept our freezer full of wild game and as my sons came along, we have had to buy more freezers to keep up with the amount of venison harvested each year. I have loved living off of the harvested venison and enjoy the exceptional depth of flavor that it offers not to mention not having to buy meat at the supermarket.

There are a few reasons for the tough texture and gamey taste of venison. Deer, unlike domesticated cattle, have to rely on the vegetation in the wild for survival and on average are older when harvested. They are lean from their diet and exercise, therefore do not have the marbling of fat that beef contains. Although this makes the beef healthier, it also can cause the meat to be tough if it is not prepared properly. The deer's diet along with improper aging will cause venison to taste gamey. Venison does have a distinct flavor just as grass fed beef has a distinct flavor and this must not be confused with gaminess. Most domestic raised animals are bred to be tasteless and fatty. Venison has much more depth of flavor than beef and if properly prepared will be incredibly and delectably tender.

If a walk-in cooler is not available, it is best to quickly process your venison, then allow the meat to age in the refrigerator on a rack, not allowing it to sit in its blood, for 5 to 7 days. Once it has been aged, package the cuts of meat in a double wrap of butcher paper or vacuum sealed bags, then label and date the packages. If you have a walk in freezer, hang it and leave it for 7 to 10 days. Following these simple steps should rid the venison of any undesirable gamey flavors.

I prepare the various cuts of venison using different methods. Just as our ancestors before us, I braise the shoulder and neck and use them in stews and soups, brown the loin in a super hot skillet and serving it rare, and prepare the hindquarter roast in a diversity of ways. Since venison does not have much fat, I add healthy fats such as olive oil when I brown the meat. This adds any necessary fat that allows for more tenderness and juiciness to the venison.

Additional to the exceptional taste of venison, the health benefits far outweigh those of beef. Not only is deer a free-ranging consumer of healthy herbs, grasses, acorns, berries, and nuts and exempt from harmful antibiotics and harmful hormones, its meat is lower in fat and cholesterol and is higher in vitamin B6, B12, and Omega 3 fatty acids. Many people are choosing to take their health in to their own hands beginning with the foods they eat. They are paying high prices to obtain naturally grass fed meat and many are hunting to acquire meat for their tables in the natural state that God intended.

Venison is that meat of any game animal, especially that of a deer. My venison recipes are suitable to whitetail, red deer, fallow deer, moose, caribou, and pronghorn antelope.

I find that preparing for and hunting wild game has contributed to the closeness of our family. As our family plans the hunt, prepare the fields, and plant nutritious vegetation for the animals in the wild, much fun, conversation, and ideas abound. Each person contributes to the family's sustenance whether it is to gather or hunt, or whether it is to prepare and cook the venison. It is all an adventure for every age whether male, female, old, or young.

There are no phones, gadgets, or distractions; just you, the kids, and the great outdoors. After the meal is prepared, the stories come to life of the hunt, and all the preparation and hard work together is rewarded with a delicious, succulent meal. Enjoy your family as you begin or continue the family traditions of planning, working, hunting, and enjoying the outdoors and the incredible food that you harvest together.

Moroccan Venison Shepherd's Pie

Sweet potatoes are about the easiest vegetables in the world to grow if you can keep the deer away from them. During late summer, does with fawns find them irresistible. The Moroccan spices and the sweet potatoes make this dish flavorful and exciting.

Ingredients

2 tablespoons olive oil
1½ pounds venison hindquarter, cut into 1-inch cubes
½ teaspoon roasted ground cumin
½ teaspoon kosher salt
1 onion, chopped
4 cloves garlic, minced
1 tablespoon tomato paste
2 cups beef broth
⅓ cup black olives
⅓ cup raisins
3 tablespoons honey
½ teaspoon ground red pepper
¼ teaspoon ground turmeric
½ teaspoon cinnamon, divided
1 cup frozen green peas
4 cups sweet potatoes, peeled and chopped
1 large egg, lightly beaten

Preheat oven to 350 degrees. Heat oil in a medium-sized skillet over medium high heat. Sprinkle venison with cumin and salt. Add venison to the pan and brown for about 1 minute on each side. Remove venison from the pan. Add onions and sauté for 3 minutes. Add garlic for about 30 seconds, and then add the tomato paste. Stir well.

Add broth to the pan. Bring to a boil, scraping pan to loosen the browned bits. Stir in olives, raisins, honey, ground red pepper, turmeric, and one half of the cinnamon. Add venison back to the pan. Reduce heat, and simmer 30 minutes. Remove from heat and stir in the peas.

Meanwhile, place sweet potatoes in a pot of boiling water until tender and drain. Sprinkle with a pinch of salt and the rest of the cinnamon. Beat potatoes with a mixer and add egg. Continue mixing until well combined. Spoon venison mixture evenly into a pie dish, and then spread potato mixture over the venison mixture. If you want to make it extra special for company, cut the end off of a gallon zip top bag, place a cake frosting tip on the end, spoon the sweet potatoes into the bag and decorate the top of the venison mixture completely with the sweet potatoes. Place the dish on a baking sheet and bake at 350 degrees for 30 minutes or until bubbly.

Easy Venison Chili Con Carne

Serves 6 to 8

Everyone has their favorite chili recipe and this is my family's favorite. Venison chili adds a depth of flavor that is superior to other kids of meats. President Johnson knew this and it is noted that he requested the cooks at the White House to use only venison for his chili. The corn mix in this recipe adds an earthy flavor and adds a texture that is perfect for Con Carne.

Ingredients

1 16-ounce can of tomatoes, diced
3 teaspoons minced canned chipotle chili in adobe sauce
5 slices bacon, finely chopped
4 pounds venison stew meat, cut into ½-inch cubes
Kosher salt and pepper
2 tablespoons olive oil
1 large onion, chopped
1 jalapeño chili, seeded and chopped
1 can kidney beans
3 tablespoons chili powder
1½ teaspoons ground cumin
1½ teaspoon oregano
4 garlic cloves, minced
4 cups beef broth
1 tablespoon packed brown sugar
2 tablespoons yellow corn mix

Always make sure your venison is dry and the skillet is super hot before you brown the meat. Browning enhances the flavor of the dish by giving more depth of flavor.

In a food processor, place tomatoes and chipotle chili and puree until smooth (This should only take about 10 seconds). In a Dutch oven, cook the bacon over medium heat until crisp. Transfer bacon to paper towel. Leave the fat in the pan.

Pat venison dry and season with salt and pepper. Heat the fat until smoking hot. Brown half of the venison. (Do not crowd the pan or the meat will steam instead of brown). This should take about 6 to 8 minutes. Using a slotted spoon, transfer to bowl and repeat.

Add the olive oil, onions, and jalapeño to Dutch oven and cook for about 5 minutes or until softened. Stir in kidney beans, chili powder, cumin, oregano, and garlic.

Cook for about 30 seconds. Stir in broth, tomato mixture and brown sugar and bring to a boil. Reduce heat to low and simmer, covered, for 1 hour. Uncover and simmer for about 30 minutes longer.

Ladle 1 cup chili liquid into medium-sized bowl and stir in yellow corn mix. Whisk mixture into chili and simmer until chili thickens. Check seasonings. Serve with a dollop of sour cream or cheese and Jalapeño Cornbread (page 56).

On our honeymoon, we went skiing in Jackson Hole, Wyoming. What an adventure. We loved the food, and both gained about 10 pounds in that 1 week. One thing that I noticed was that most of the restaurants had some kind of wild game on their menu, namely venison. That amazed me. I thought cooking venison was just what "good ole' boy" Southern hunters cooked. I never knew that it could be an ELAGANT DELICACY. The other thing I noticed was that it was expensive: PEOPLE WANTED IT. I was inspired to learn how to make it a delicacy in my home. One morning, we had breakfast at this awesome restaurant where we had to wait about 2-hours to get in. I loved this dish and wanted to replicate it at home. I think I've got it pretty close.

Western Venison Open-Faced Sandwich with Fried Egg

Serves 6

Venison Ingredients

1½ pounds venison hindquarter roast, sliced in half horizontally
4 tablespoons olive oil, extra for browning
1 Vidalia onion, chopped
2 cloves of garlic
1 pound tomatoes, peeled or canned with their juices
1 tablespoon tomato paste
3 tablespoons fresh basil, chopped
Kosher salt
Freshly ground pepper
4 eggs
4 slices of artisan bread, cut ½ inch thick toasted or grilled
6 tablespoons butter
4 tablespoons Parmesan-Reggiano cheese
¼ cup parsley

Marinade Ingredients

¼ cup rosemary
¼ cup thyme
½ cup olive oil
3 cloves garlic

For marinade, mix rosemary, thyme, olive oil, garlic and venison in a zip top bag and refrigerate 4 hours.

Remove venison from refrigerator and pound each half to ¾ inch thick. Season liberally with salt and pepper. Heat 2 tablespoons of olive oil in a medium- size skillet over medium-high heat until skillet is almost smoking and oil is shimmering. Place venison in skillet for about 4 minutes on the first side, then turn over and cook for 3 to 4 minutes. Transfer to cooling rack and allow to rest.

Meanwhile, heat 2 tablespoons of oil in a medium sized saucepan over medium-high. Add onions and garlic and stir for 30 seconds. Add tomatoes, tomato paste, basil, ½ teaspoon of salt, and ¼ teaspoon of pepper. Bring mixture to a boil, then reduce it to a simmer for about 15 minutes.

Half each piece of toast on the bias and drizzle with olive oil. Place toast on the plates.

Slice venison against the grain and distribute equally over the toast. Spoon about ¼-cup of the tomato mixture over the venison.

Heat 2 tablespoons of olive oil in a non-stick skillet over medium heat. Add 3 eggs at one time to the pan. Cover and cook at medium to medium-low heat for 2-3 minutes or until whites are set, but yolk is still soft. Gently remove the eggs from the skillet and place over the tomatoes. Repeat with remaining eggs.

Sprinkle 1 tablespoon of Parmesan-Reggiano cheese over the egg. Garnish with Parsley and serve immediately.

Stuffed Venison Meatloaf

Serves 6

This dish is so beautiful in its presentation that it's hard to call it a comfort meal. It's one of the most elegant and easy comfort dishes that I've ever made, and is always a winner in our home.

Ingredients

2 teaspoons olive oil
1 onion, chopped
2 garlic cloves, chopped
2 carrots, julienned
1 pound ground venison
1 pound ground lean beef
2 cups bread crumbs
1 cup Parmesan-Reggiano cheese
2 teaspoons Dijon mustard
3 large eggs, lightly beaten
1 tablespoon kosher salt
½ tablespoon pepper
15-20 spinach leaves
4 ounces mozzarella cheese, thinly sliced
10 slices no-nitrate bacon

Preheat oven to 400 degrees. Heat olive oil in 10-inch skillet over medium heat. Put onions into skillet and sweat the onions until softened. Add garlic and cook for 30 seconds.

Bring a stockpot of water to a boil. Add carrots to the water and boil them for 8 minutes. Drain and set aside.

In a large bowl, combine ground venison, beef, breadcrumbs, softened onions, garlic, Parmesan-Reggiano, Dijon mustard, eggs, salt and pepper.

Form the meat mixture into a ½ inch thick, 10x16 inch rectangle on a Silpat or piece of wax paper. Lay the spinach leaves over the meat leaving a ½ inch border around the perimeter of the rectangle. Layer Mozzarella slices on top of basil leaves and then lay the carrots lengthwise on top of the Mozzarella. Roll the meat lengthwise (starting with long side) making it as tight as possible. Pick up Silpat or wax paper and roll the loaf onto a rack that is placed on top of a half sheet pan with sides.

Slice bacon in half and place width wise over the loaf. Bake for 1 hour or until loaf reaches 165 degrees.

Transfer the meatloaf to a cutting board. Cut meatloaf into 1" slices and serve with Garlic Mashed Potatoes (page 76), salad, and crusty bread.

Ragu Bolognese

Serves 4 to 6

There are some great dishes you can make ahead of time, freeze, and use when convenient. Bolognese is one of these dishes. I like to make a triple batch of the sauce, have some for dinner, and freeze the other two batches for another time.

Ingredients

¼ cup extra virgin olive oil
2 medium onions, finely chopped
4 ribs celery, finely chopped
2 carrots, finely chopped
4 cloves garlic, sliced
1 pound ground venison
1 pound ground beef
4 ounces slab bacon, finely chopped
2 16-ounce cans of tomatoes, crushed (preferably homemade)
2 tablespoons tomato paste
1 teaspoon fresh thyme leaves
1 cup dry red wine
½ cup heavy cream
¼ teaspoon nutmeg
Kosher salt and freshly ground pepper
1 box fettuccine noodles
½ cup Parmesan cheese, plus extra for serving

Heat olive oil in a heavy-bottomed pot over medium heat until hot. Add the onions, celery, carrots, and garlic and cook for 5 minutes or until vegetables are translucent.

Increase the heat and add venison, beef, and bacon, stirring often.

Add tomatoes, tomato paste, wine, and thyme. Bring to a boil, then lower to a simmer for 1 hour.

Meanwhile, bring a large pot of water to a boil. Add 1 tablespoon of oil and 1 tablespoon of salt to the water. Add Fettuccine to the water for about 12 minutes or until al dente.

Add heavy cream and nutmeg to the sauce. Simmer about 8 to 10 minutes. Season with salt and pepper to taste. Remove from heat, and let cool.

When the pasta is cooked, drain and place the noodles on 4 to 5 plates. Top the pasta with the sauce. Divide the Parmesan cheese among the plates and serve.

Venison Korean Wraps

Serves 6

I love the flavors in these super wraps! The spicy, salty, flavor of the venison paired with the sweet cabbage dressing and Taco Sauce is perfectly balanced. The cabbage adds just enough crunch and texture to make this dish absolutely addictive.

Ingredients

8 tablespoons soy sauce, divided
6 teaspoons toasted sesame oil, divided
1½ teaspoons salt
¼ pepper
4 tablespoons honey, divided
2 tablespoons lime juice
2 tablespoons hoisin sauce
1 tablespoon red pepper paste
1 teaspoon rice wine vinegar
2 garlic cloves, smashed
1½ pounds venison hindquarter, sliced in half horizontally
12 mini flour tortillas
4 cups shredded iceberg lettuce
¼ cup shredded Napa cabbage
¼ cup shredded red cabbage
10 scallions, sliced on the bias

For marinade, combine 5 tablespoons soy sauce, 2 teaspoons of sesame oil, salt, and pepper in a medium bowl. Coat the venison with the marinade. Cover and refrigerate for at least 1 hour.

Meanwhile, prepare the Cabbage Dressing and the Korean Taco Sauce. For the Cabbage Dressing, combine 1 tablespoon soy sauce, 1 tablespoon honey, 2 teaspoons sesame oil, and lime juice in a large bowl. Mix well and set aside.

For the Korean Taco Sauce, combine 2 tablespoons soy sauce, the 3 remaining tablespoons honey, 2 teaspoons sesame oil, hoisin sauce, red pepper paste, rice wine vinegar, and garlic in a medium bowl.

Remove venison from refrigerator. Heat cast iron skillet until smoking hot, and then add both pieces of venison. Brown for 3 minutes. Turn over for another 2 to 3 minutes until medium rare. Transfer venison to a cutting board and let rest.

Meanwhile, place 3 tortillas in a large, dry, non-stick skillet over medium-high heat until pliable, about 20 seconds per side. Repeat with remaining tortillas.

Add lettuce, cabbage, and scallions to bowl with Cabbage Dressing. Toss to combine. Add salt and pepper to taste.

Cut venison into strips across the bias.

Fill tortillas with cabbage mixture, venison, and drizzle with Korean Taco Sauce.

Chili Cocoa Crusted Venison with Berry Reduction

Serves 6

Chocolate is amazingly awesome with venison, believe it or not. Well, chocolate on almost anything is irresistible. I knew Scott was the man for me when he was able to resist Alaskan chocolate covered berries after losing 20 pounds in 2 weeks on an Alaskan hunting trip just to bring me my favorite ingredient and treat!

Ingredients

⅓ cup coffee grounds
¼ cup cocoa
2½ tablespoon salt
1 tablespoon brown sugar
1 teaspoon cinnamon
½ teaspoon cayenne pepper
½ venison loin
olive oil for browning

It is known that melting chocolate in your mouth increases brain activity and prevents potential brain problems in the elderly.

Preheat oven to 350 degrees.

In a medium sized bowl, mix coffee grounds, cocoa, salt, brown sugar, cinnamon, and cayenne pepper in a bowl. Rub mixture into loin.

Heat cast iron skillet to almost smoking. Place loin into skillet and brown on all sides.

Place loin in 350-degree oven 4 to 5 minutes, depending on size of loin. Remove to a cutting board. Let rest for at least 5 minutes.

Slice into 1-inch pieces on a platter and spoon berry reduction on top of venison. Serve with collard greens.

BERRY REDUCTION

1½ cups blackberries
½ cup blueberries
½ cup red wine (cabernet-sauvignon)
¼ cup sugar
1 lemon, juiced
Kosher salt, to taste

Place blackberries, blueberries, red wine, sugar, and lemon juice in a small saucepan and bring to a boil. Reduce the heat to simmer and reduce by half. Season with salt.

Venison Burrito Supreme

Serves 4

This recipe is not only one of the tastiest burrito recipes I have eaten, it is healthy as well. My family devours these burritos the minute they are made. These burritos are easy to make and if you are having a party everyone can have fun creating their own! Be sure to double the Tomatillo Sauce and the Pico de Gallo and use it for chip dipping.

Ingredients

4 tablespoons olive oil
4 garlic cloves
1½ teaspoons red pepper flakes
1 jar black beans (16oz.)
1 pound venison hindquarter
Salt and pepper to taste
1½ cups cooked rice
4 flour tortillas
6 tablespoons chopped cilantro

Pico de Gallo

2 tablespoons chopped cilantro
4 plum tomatoes, cored and chopped
½ red onion, minced
1 jalapeño chili, seeded and minced
1 tablespoon lime juice

Combine Pico de Gallo ingredients in medium bowl and season with salt and pepper. Set aside.

Heat 2 tablespoons of olive oil in large saucepan over medium-high heat until just smoking. Add garlic and red pepper flakes and brown for about 30 seconds. Add beans, bring to a boil, and then reduce it to a simmer for about 15 minutes. Season with salt and pepper.

Meanwhile, prepare the tomatillo sauce (page 126).

Slice hindquarter venison in half horizontally. Pound each half to about 3/4 inches thick. Season liberally with salt and pepper. Heat oil in a large skillet over medium high heat until skillet is smoking hot. Place venison in skillet for about 4 minutes on the first side, turn and cook the other side for 3 to 4 minutes. Transfer to a cutting board, tent with foil, and let rest 5 minutes.

Slice steaks thinly against the grain. Place tortillas on 4 plates and evenly divide rice, beans, venison, and Pico de Gallo among them. Fold tortillas to form burritos. Spoon Tomatillo sauce on top of burrito and garnish with cilantro. Serve immediately.

Beer-Braised Venison with Turnips, Onions, and Carrots

Serves 4 to 6

During hunting season, we always plant turnips in our green fields for the deer. The great thing about this is that we enjoy cooking them with the game we harvest! Not only are there many gastronomic benefits of turnips, the health benefits seem endless. Turnips are filled with antioxidants, are rich in vitamins C, A, K, B, folic acid, and carotenoids. Next time you feel a cold coming on, eat some turnips and enjoy this hearty tasty stew.

Ingredients

1 pound venison hindquarter roast
½ teaspoon freshly ground black pepper
1½ tablespoons salt
½ cup all-purpose flour
3 tbsp. olive oil
1 cup beef broth
4 garlic cloves, crushed
1 (12 ounce) dark beer
2 bay leaves
4 carrots, peeled and cut diagonally into ½-inch thick slices
10 ounces small turnips, peeled and cut into wedges
1 large onion, peeled and cut into wedges
¼ cup chopped fresh flat-leaf parsley

Cut hindquarter into 1-inch cubes. Place them in a medium sized bowl. Sprinkle salt and pepper liberally over meat. Mix well. Coat the meat with the flour.

Heat oil in a Dutch oven. When smoking hot, brown meat on all sides. Do not crowd the pan; If necessary, brown meat in batches.

Add beef broth, beer, and garlic cloves and bay leaves. Scrape the browned bits off of the bottom of the pan and bring to a boil.

Add carrots, turnips, and onion to Dutch oven. Bring to a boil. Once it reaches a boil, bring heat down to a simmer and cook covered for about an hour.

Sprinkle parsley on top and serve over mashed potatoes and crusty bread.

Venison Lettuce Wraps

On days I feel like having a light meal I prepare these little jewels. They are so full of flavor and texture. You get salty, sweet and crunch! The kids start piling into the kitchen as the aromas of the dish reach their noses. The wraps hardly make it to the table.

Ingredients

1 pound venison hindquarter, diced into ½-inch cubes
2 tablespoons soy sauce
1 teaspoon red pepper flakes
1 tablespoon hoisin sauce
2 tablespoons lemon juice
¼ cup peanut oil
2 cups diced water chestnuts
½ cup diced white onions
1 cup diced green onions
1 garlic clove, smashed
1 teaspoon fresh-smashed ginger
1 tablespoon seasoned rice wine vinegar
3 tablespoons soy sauce
3 tablespoons chicken stock
1 head iceberg lettuce, washed and separated

Peanut oil has a high heat tolerance. The oil is less likely to burn at high temperatures.

To make this dish extra special, fry some rice sticks in peanut oil until puffed and serve on top of lettuce wraps. They can be found in the Asian isle of the grocery store.

Mix soy sauce, red pepper flakes, hoisin sauce, and lemon juice in a medium bowl. Marinate venison in mixture for 20 minutes.

Heat peanut oil in a wok. When oil is shimmering add ½ of the marinated meat and brown. Transfer first batch of meat to a plate and repeat with remaining half.

Add water chestnuts, white onions, green onions, garlic, and ginger to wok for 2 to 3 minutes.

Add vinegar, soy sauce, and chicken stock until caramelized.

Place venison in the wok with the onion mixture. Mix well.

Serve in lettuce leaves.

Venison Scaloppine

Serves 6

Scaloppine is an elegant, but simple dish to prepare. The flavor and texture of venison prepared as scaloppine can't be matched.

Ingredients

1½ pounds venison loin
2 cups all purpose flour
2 teaspoons kosher salt
1 teaspoon freshly ground black pepper
3 extra large eggs
2 cups breadcrumbs, dried and seasoned
1 pound large button mushrooms, quartered
1½ cups sherry or marsala wine
4 tablespoons cold unsalted butter
3 tablespoons fresh thyme leaves

Slice venison into 1-inch pieces. Pound to ¼ inch thick.

On a plate, mix together flour, salt, and pepper. On a second plate, beat the eggs with 1 tablespoon of water. On a third plate, add the breadcrumbs.

Lightly dredge venison in the flour mixture, then the eggs, and lastly the breadcrumbs.

Heat oil and half the butter in a large cast iron skillet or sauté pan. Cook about 2 minutes over medium heat on each side or until brown. Transfer pieces of venison to a cooling rack.

Add a little more olive oil and the mushrooms to the pan until juices have been absorbed. Add sherry to mushrooms and reduce by half. Add remaining butter to the pan and bring just to a boil. Lower the heat to medium and cook for about 5 more minutes.

Stir in the thyme leaves. Pour mushrooms and sauce over the venison and serve.

Make a double match of the fried venison, freeze one batch on sheet pans until frozen, then store it in freezer bags. When ready to use it, remove from freezer and place on a baking sheet and bake at 200 degrees until warmed through. Meanwhile, prepare the sauce and serve with your favorite crusty bread.

The Lost Art *of* Sausage Making

Making sausage yourself truly has become a lost art. Most people are satisfied to pick up a pack of Kielbasa from their local store and stick to those flavors as opposed to creating their very own flavor profiles. I have nothing against Kielbasa sausage. It really is fantastic, but knowing just how easy making sausage can be and that I get to determine every aspect of the recipe gives me the incentive I need to get out my fresh meat and CREATE!

Venison is described as any game animal killed by hunting. Originally, you would categorize rabbit, pig, and even goats as venison. Here, in America, when we refer to venison, primarily we are speaking of deer including antelope, elk, caribou, whitetail deer, and the like. Keep that in mind as you read this article. Although I am using whitetail deer for my sausage recipes, feel free to substitute that meat with whatever meat you may have.

Venison Sausage is one of those "must haves" if you frequently dine on venison. In most hunting circles, just mentioning venison sausage gives a nostalgic feeling of waking up to a venison sausage breakfast at the hunting camp after an enjoyable weekend of hunting. Every hunter needs to have in his skills set the ability to make his own sausage. It is really very simple. Many people believe that it is too time consuming or that they would rather leave that to the processor, but each of us are individuals with a variety of tastes and with just a little knowledge, you can make your own sausage to your liking with little effort and a super tasty reward.

Through the years of speaking on the subject of eating wild, I get to meet resourceful farmers, hunters, gardeners, and wild life enthusiasts. In the past few years, I have noticed that more and more of them are beginning to process their own deer and therefore, are looking for tools and recipes to make their processing easier. You can order almost all of the necessary tools right off the internet. Equipment may be as minimal as a manual meat grinder depending upon whether you want to make breakfast sausage, link sausage, smoked sausage, or cured sausage.

EQUIPMENT

First, you need a meat grinder. You can use your stand mixer with the meat grinder attachments, a manual grinder, or you can go all out and buy an electric meat grinder. My family of 9 usually harvests about 13 deer a year, therefore we process quite a lot of venison. Our investment in a meat grinder has certainly brought a tremendous return. If you are going to be processing more than a deer or two a year, I suggest that you buy at least an ½ horsepower grinder. They are faster and much more quiet than the lower horsepower grinders.

If you are going to make links, you will need casings. There are all kinds of casings out there, but I find that natural hog or sheep casing are the best for the money. Nothing is quite like using a natural casing. The natural casings "snap" when you bite into them and help to create a beautiful color to the sausage.

You don't have to have a sausage stuffer and I didn't for a long time, but I do think it is easier and more convenient to have one. Sometimes, using only the grinder attachment cause the sausage to get too hot resulting in a sub par texture. They can be expensive, but if you are planning on making sausage often, the investment is worth it.

If you plan on smoking your sausage, you will need a smoker. You can purchase these at your local sporting good store or make one yourself. This winter, I am planning on building a smoke house to cold smoke my sausage, but for now, I am completely satisfied hot smoking. Dry sausages such as summer sausage, pepperoni and salami are cold smoked and requires temperatures below 60 degrees for about 15 to 48 hours or longer for desired flavor and dryness. Cold smoking allows total smoke penetration inside the meat and has a very long shelf life. Using curing salts, drying, and cold smoking meats are a very effective and tasty way to preserve meats.

Hot smoking relies on a humidity and heat balance to get that great smoky flavor. Placing a liquid filled pan (I like to use apple juice) inside of a small smoker and wetting wood chips an hour before smoking will help regulate the temperature inside. I prefer using a propane smoker in that I am able to control the temperature to a greater degree than with an electric smoker, and the propane smoker reaches temperature faster. Hot smoking dries out the surface of the meat creating a barrier for smoke penetration, but allowing enough smoke flavor to create great sausage in a relatively short amount of time. Hot smoked meats should be kept in the refrigerator and if not consumed fairly quickly, they should be frozen.

When smoking links, allow the links to dry for an hour or two before putting them in the smoker. Smoke the links for about 3 hours, maybe longer if they have not reached an internal temperature of 150-160 degrees. I usually remove the wood chips after the first hour and one-half and continue to maintain the temperature in the smoker until the desired internal temperature is reached. You can remove the sausage from the smoker and finish them in a 200 degree oven if this works better for you. Allow them to cool before freezing.

MAKING GOOD SAUSAGE

Good sausage is a result of fresh ingredients and proper balance. Venison is quite lean and needs a little fat, liquid, salt, and herbs and spices to create a super sausage. Once you have the right balance of ingredients the sky's the limit. I like to use pork, beef, or lamb along with my venison in sausages, but this is not necessary. I do recommend using fat back if you aren't going to use multiple meats as venison can be a little dry by itself. Here are a few basic sausage making steps that will give you a leg-up on sausage making.

1. Everything that you are going to be using to make your sausage, such as bowls, feeder for the grinder, stuffer, meat, and fat needs to be cold-very cold. If your ingredients get warm, your sausage mixture is going to get mushy. I suggest putting all your equipment, venison, and fat in the freezer for about an hour before using them.

2. Before removing your ingredients from the freezer, make certain that you have all your spices ready to go into your mixture. You are going to need to work fast so that your meat remains cold.

3. Remove only your meat from the freezer and cut meat and fat into 1-inch cubes. Mix with your dry ingredients, cover, and place back into the freezer along with any liquid that is to go into the recipe back into the freezer for 30 minutes.

4. After your sausage mixture has chilled, remove equipment, and ingredients from the freezer and set up your work station.

5. If you making link sausage, soak your casings in warm water to remove the salt and to soften them. I like to use 32 – 36 mm casings. If you aren't making link sausage, ignore this step.

6. Add the liquid to your chilled sausage mixture and blend with your hands. Attach the ⅜-inch plate (course or largest die) to the grinder and begin feeding the mixture. By using this plate, you have less chance of your sausage becoming mushy. If your mixture feels warm, place it back into the freezer for a few minutes while you attach the stuffer to the grinder and clean up a bit.

If you are not stuffing your sausage, freeze as if you were freezing ground venison or prepare patties, freeze on a cookie sheet, place wax paper between the patties, and place in a freezer bag. Give them a night in the refrigerator if you are planning on eating them fresh; the flavors will then have been infused into the meat.

7. Place a casing onto the stuffing tube leaving about 5 to 6 inches off the end of the tub to tie off; air will fill some of that casing. Feed the mixture into the stuffer. Allow the sausage come out in one long coil trying to keep the sausage casing consistent in size as it continues to come out of the tube. Remember to leave about 8-inches extra casing after the last of the sausage is stuffed. Tie off the casing in a knot.

8. If desired, every 5-inches or so, pinch off what will become the links. Roll the link a few times and repeat until you get to the end of the sausage. Tie off the other end. Arrange the links on a wire or cooling sheets where air can move around them. Allow the sausage to dry for about an hour. If you are smoking them, place them in the smoker, but if you are freezing them, refrigerate overnight then dry and package them for the freezer. If you are going to eat them, they will keep in the refrigerator for up to a week.

One of my very favorite link sausages to make is Italian Sausage. It is a wonderful sausage to smoke, grill, or fry. I personally like Italian Sausage fried with onions, and bell peppers. It is great on a bun or on top of greens, grits, or mashed potatoes. The versatility of Italian Sausage amazes me. Oftentimes, I will remove the casing and add it to my pizza or spaghetti sauce.

If you try any sausage recipe at all, this one is a must. I like to smoke mine before cooking. It seems to add an earthy element to the sausage that I can't get any other way. When in a fix, marinade your sausage in a dark beer. I like cooking with Guinness beer. If you don't want to use beer, you can brush a very small amount of liquid smoke over the sausage links before grilling, baking, or frying them.

Italian Venison Sausage

Ingredients

2 ½ pounds ground venison
2 ½ pounds ground pork
2 tablespoons Kosher salt
1 teaspoon sugar
1 ½ tablespoons fennel seeds, cracked
1 teaspoon coriander
⅜ cup cold water
1 ½ tablespoon cayenne pepper
1 teaspoon fresh rosemary, chopped

Chill attachments, venison, and pork in the freezer for about an hour. Remove meat from the freezer and cut into 1-inch strips. Mix dry ingredients into the mixture, cover, and return to the freezer for about 30 minutes.

Meanwhile, if you are going to make link sausage soak the casings in warm water to remove the salt and soften the casings. You can run water through the casings to make sure there are no holes in them.

Remove equipment and ingredients from the freezer and quickly set up for grinding the meat. Add cold water to the meat and spices and mix with your hands. Place the ⅜-inch plate on the grinder and begin feeding the mixture through the feeder.

If you are not making link sausage, you can freeze the sausage as you would ground venison. To make the link sausage, place a casing onto the stuffer leaving 6 inches of casing for tying off. Begin stuffing the sausage into the casing leaving about 8 inches to tie off the end of the casing. If you have remaining sausage, use it as patties or ground sausage. Tie off the casing in a knot.

If desired, every 5-inches or so, pinch off what will become the links. Roll the link a few times and repeat until you get to the end of the sausage. Tie off the other end. Arrange the links on a wire or cooling sheets where air can move around them. Allow the sausage to dry for about an hour. Freeze, cook, or smoke the sausage and enjoy!

If you have never made sausage before, breakfast sausage is a great place to start. You can use any mixture of spices that you like. Traditionally breakfast sausage consists of sage, rosemary, thyme, nutmeg, red pepper flakes, salt, and pepper. I have created a simple recipe that my family loves with very few ingredients. I often make link sausage with this recipe and save some of the mixture back for a few servings of breakfast sausage as well. You can freeze this mixture as you would ground venison and bring it out for your favorite Italian dish, use in soups, and meatballs.

Breakfast Sausage

Serves 8

Hint: if your venison is already ground, just chop the pancetta in very small pieces and add to your ground venison.

Ingredients

4 pounds of venison scraps (you could use any part of the deer for this recipe), run through the largest holes of the meat grinder.
2 pounds of pancetta run through the same grinder. Have your butcher run it through his grinder if you do not have one of your own.
1 tablespoon salt
½ tablespoon pepper
½ tablespoon red pepper flakes
½ cup dry white wine
2 tablespoons extra virgin olive oil

In a large bowl, mix venison and pancetta with your hands until blended. Add salt, pepper, red pepper flakes, and white wine. Chill for about 30 minutes.

Form sausage into 4-ounce patties. Do not over-handle the mix as this can affect the texture of the sausage.

Heat olive oil in 10-12" cast iron skillet. Add sausage patties and cook over low heat, turning frequently, until light brown on all sides. Cook in batches. Serve with Homemade Biscuits (page 121).

What better comfort food for the Southerner than sausage and grits with an onion and tomato reduction? The creamy grits and spicy venison link sausage bring back the calm gentle days of childhood and gives me the desire to create the same memories for future generations. This recipe will hopefully stay in my family as well as yours as a keepsake. This sausage recipe can be used for sausage patties, as well as link sausage. Lasagna, spaghetti, or Bolognese can be greatly enhanced by using the sausage part of this recipe.

Many people think of sausage and grits as a winter time meal, but chilies and spicy dishes always have been used in the heat to cause perspiration to cool oneself down. Fresh tomatoes picked right off the vine can't be matched for taste and freshness during the hot south summer. This is a dish you will love to eat anytime of the year.

You can use any cut of the deer for this recipe.

Venison Sausage Smothered *in* Italian Tomatoes *and* Onions Over Cheesy Grits

Serves 8

THE SAUSAGE

4 pounds venison scraps, run through the largest holes of grinder.
2 pounds of lean bacon (no nitrates), run through the same grinder.
1 tablespoon kosher salt
½ tablespoon pepper
½ tablespoon red pepper flakes
1 tablespoon rosemary, minced
½ cup Italian parsley
½ cup dry white wine
8 ounces sausage casings (about 8 feet)

Directions

In a large bowl, mix the venison and bacon with your hands until well blended. Add the rest of the ingredients and mix just until blended. Chill mixture for 30 minutes.

Set up a sausage stuffer and attach the casing to the funnel feeder. Begin stuffing the sausage into the casing and twist every 4 inches. Keep the diameter about 1 inch to insure proper cooking. Prick sausage with a pin all over. Chill until ready to cook.

FOR TOMATO AND ONION SAUCE

3 tablespoons extra virgin olive oil
1 medium yellow onion, ½ inch diced
2 cloves garlic, minced
2 tablespoons tomato paste
½ cup chicken stock
1 cup red wine
¼ cup Italian parsley

Heat 2 tablespoons of olive oil in 10 to 12 inch sauté pan. Add half the sausage links to the pan. Cook over low heat, turning frequently, until browned on all sides. Transfer to a plate. Brown remaining sausage links and transfer to plate.

Pour 1 tablespoon olive oil in the same pan sausage was cooked. Add onions and garlic to the pan and cook until soft, 8 to 10 minutes.

In a small bowl mix tomato paste, stock, and red wine and mix well. Add mixture to the pan. Scrape brown bits from the bottom of the pan and bring to a simmer.

Return sausage to the pan, cover, and cook for 15 minutes or until cooked through. Stir in parsley and serve over Cheesy Grits (page 165).

Stuffed Venison Loin

Serves 8

Stuffed venison loin is a tender, tasty, easy, elegant dish. It is perfect for special occasions. It's very versatile in taste. You could add mushrooms, different cheeses and herbs. It allows for creativity in a consistent no fail dish!

Ingredients

2 venison loins, butterflied
½ cup breadcrumbs
¾ cup shredded mozzarella cheese
1 cup Parmesan cheese
½ cup olive oil
½ cup chopped basil leaves
2 garlic cloves, minced
Kosher Salt
Pepper

In a medium sized bowl, mix together breadcrumbs, cheeses, olive oil, basil, and garlic.

Preheat oven to 350 degrees. Butterfly the two loins.

Spread filling evenly over the loin. Roll up the loin and truss. Liberally sprinkle with salt and pepper. Place in smoking hot cast iron skillet. Brown loins on all sides. Place loins in 350-degree oven for 3 to 4 minutes. Remove from pan. Let rest. Slice into 1-inch pieces.

Serve with Homemade Mashed Potatoes, rice, carrots, green beans, or salad.

How To Butterfly a Loin

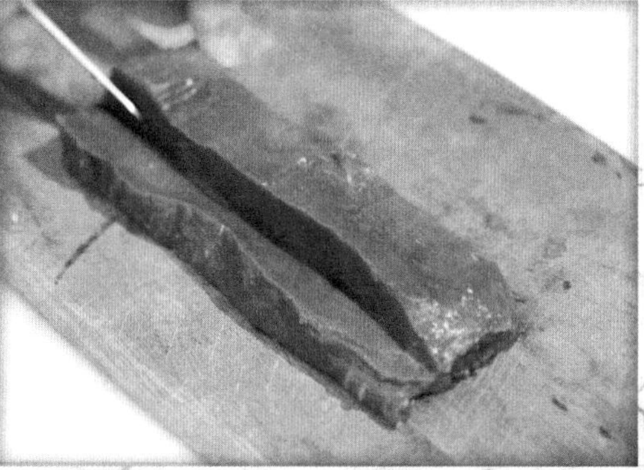

Step 1 With a long sharp knife on the right half of the loin, slice loin 2/3 of the way through.

Step 2 Turn over and repeat.

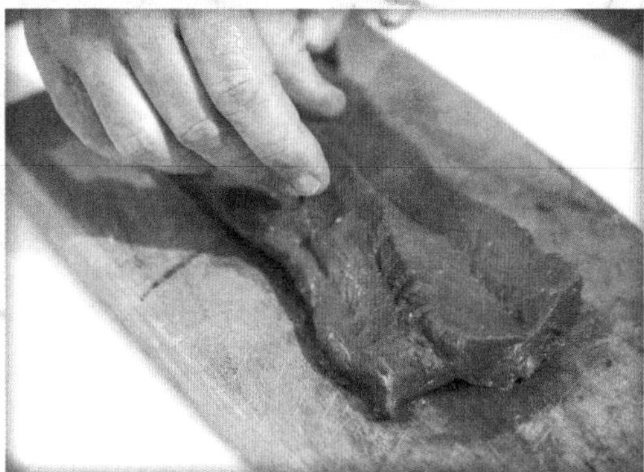

Step 3 Spread loin as flat as possible.

Step 4 Pound the loin to about ¼ inch thick.

Step 5 Completely flatten the butterflied loin and spread stuffing over the loin leaving ½-inch border around the edges. Gently roll loin in to a log and begin to truss.

How To Truss a Loin

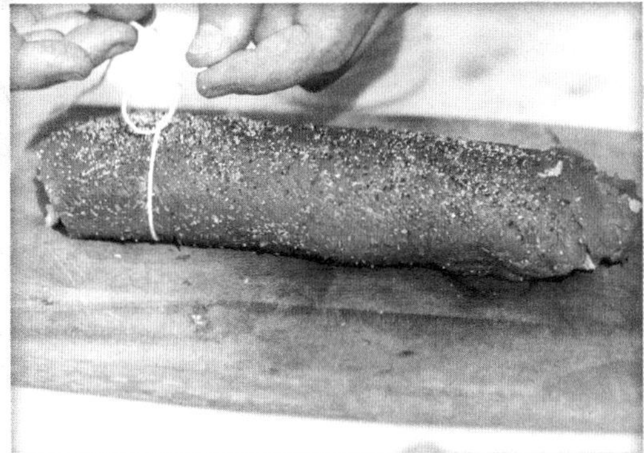

Step 1 Using butcher's twine about 6 times longer than your loin, wrap around loin approximately 1½ inches from end and tie a knot.

Step 2 Hold the short end of the twine above the knot with your left hand. Pull the long end of the twine away from you and slip it under the part of the twine that you are holding taut above the loin. Repeat wrapping process every 1½ to 2 inches until entire loin is trussed.

Step 3 Turn the loin over and stretch the twine around the end, wrapping around each truss until it reaches the first initial truss. Tie ends together and trim excess.

Wild Game Substitutions

All venison recipes succeed using beef, but not all beef recipes succeed using venison. There are many of you reading this book who do not hunt. Do not let that stop you from using the recipes in this book calling for wild game. There are substitutions that will come pretty close to the rich flavor of the proteins that are harvest from the wild. With any of your proteins, always choose grass fed organic animals and the beautiful earthy flavors will come through. Animals with a variety in their diets always taste better than those fed purely from corn or grain. My desire is that you get maximum health and flavor from your carefully chosen meats and that you never stop experimenting with your cuisine.

VENISON

In most recipes, the venison can be replaced with grass fed beef, goat, or lamb. The best cuts of meat for the various type recipes are as follows:

Venison tenderloin- beef tenderloin

Venison loin - beef loin

Venison hindquarter roast

- if used for pounded meat, stir fries, fajitas, burritos, or any other recipe that calls for slicing the meat horizontally and searing it use flank steak

- if used for braises such as stews and soups use, use beef, goat, or lamb stew meat

Ground Venison - purchase a rump roast and have the butcher grind it on the largest setting

WILD TURKEY

Domestic Turkey may be substituted for Wild Turkey. The flavor will not be as intense, but it is a good substitute.

WILD DUCK

Domestic Duck may be substituted for Wild Duck. Remove the fat from the Domestic Duck in that Wild Duck does not have the fat content that is found in Domestic ducks.

DOMESTIC POULTRY

Farm raised poultry may be substituted for domestic poultry, but the flavor will not be as intense and cut the cooking time by ⅔.

You may substitute 2 pheasants in place of domestic poultry. You can find pheasant at high end supermarkets.

QUAIL

Farm raised quail are a great substitute for wild quail. They can be found in the freezer sections of high end supermarkets. If your store does not have them, speak with the meat manager and they will probably order some for you.

Pheasant, Duck, and Quail

Slow Cooker Pheasant Nachos

Serves 8 to 10

Ingredients

¼ pound bacon (4 slices), cooked and crumbled
2 tablespoons bacon grease
1 large onion, chopped
6 garlic cloves, peeled and smashed
6 Pheasant Breasts
2 teaspoons liquid smoke
1 tablespoon Kosher salt
1 tablespoon cumin
2 tablespoons chili powder
1 teaspoon ground pepper
1 cup chicken broth
1 large bag tortilla chips
2 red or green jalapeños, sliced
Cheese Sauce (recipe below)
Guacamole (recipe below)
Bunch chives (about ¼ cup), chopped
4 ounce sour cream

In a cast iron skillet over medium heat, cook bacon for about 3 minutes and turn over and cook for another 2 to 3 minutes or until the bacon is brown. Remove to drain on a paper towel. When cool enough, crumble the bacon and set aside.

For the meat: Spread bacon grease over the bottom of the slow cooker. Place the onions and the garlic cloves in the slow cooker. In a medium bowl, add pheasant breasts, liquid smoke, salt, pepper, cumin, and chili powder and coat the pheasant with the seasoning. Place the pheasant and seasonings into the slow cooker and pour in the broth. Turn the slow cooker on low and cook for 8 hours. Once the pheasant is tender, use 2 forks to shred the meat into the juices. If you want it crispy, use a slotted spoon and scoop the meat out of the juices into a hot cast iron skillet and leave still for 2 minutes and turn.

FOR THE CHEESE SAUCE

Ingredients

3 tablespoons butter
2 tablespoons flour
1 cup warm whole milk
2 teaspoons salt
⅛ teaspoon cayenne pepper
½ teaspoon dry mustard
8 ounces extra sharp cheddar cheese, shredded

Melt the butter in a medium pan over medium heat. Once the butter is melted add the flour and whisk until the mixture is smooth and barely begins to bubble. Add the warm milk to the pan and cook over heat until it begins to boil then lower to a simmer while continuing to stir until it begins to thicken. Add the salt, cayenne, and mustard to the mixture and whisk until combined. Remove the pan from the heat and allow to cool for about 5 minutes. Add the cheese in handfuls mixing in between each handful until well incorporated and all the cheese has been added.

Pheasant Nachos are the perfect comfort meal. You can substitute chicken for the pheasant, but the pheasant's flavor is more delicate, yet deeper than that of chicken.

Pheasant has become super popular in the high-end and not-so-high-end restaurants. You can find them at local restaurant stores and in some grocery stores. If the grocery stores don't have them in stock, they can order them for you or you can order them from on-line sources. Seriously, this is an unforgettably excellent treat.

FOR THE GUACAMOLE

Ingredients

3 ripe avocados
1 jalapeño, more or less to your taste
Juice of ½ of lemon
½ onion, minced
1 medium tomato
1 teaspoon kosher salt

Mix all ingredients in medium sized bowl. Leave it a little chunky for better texture.

TO PLATE:

Sprinkle a layer of chips on a large platter. Add ½ of the cheese sauce, ½ of the guacamole, ½ of the crumbled bacon, and ½ of the chives and a few dollops of sour cream. Add another layer of chips and add the remaining ingredients in order finishing with the chives.

Duck

Throughout all the years that I have been experimenting with wild game, almost every time that I have mentioned wild duck, people have responded negatively. I almost cannot believe it. Restaurants all across the globe serve duck as one of their most beloved items. There are differences in domestic and wild ducks, and wild ducks win in flavor every time!

Wild duck do have a more intense flavor than domestic duck because they are usually older, leaner, denser, and smaller. Wild duck eat from a variety of wild foods and fly long distances using muscle and building connective tissue. This adds to the flavor of duck if prepared properly. Wild duck is easy to prepare, just a little different than domestic duck.

Dry aging is perfect for duck as well as for beef and venison. It helps to break down connective tissue and muscle fiber making the duck much more tender. Remove breasts from the bone and place duck pieces in the refrigerator lightly covered for at least 5 days. Keep the duck from sitting in its own blood by placing the duck on a cooling rack on top of a cookie sheet and draining the blood from time to time. Remove duck and freeze in airtight bags or double wrap in freezer paper. Always remember to thaw in the refrigerator.

Cooking preparation is essential to the tenderness of the duck. Many people tend to overcook wild duck. Serving duck rare is by far my favorite application, but duck can also be braised in oil. Removing the fat from wild duck and replacing it with olive oil mixed with butter gives the duck an earthy flavor, and removes the gaminess that can be distasteful. Duck hunting is incredibly fun and enjoying wild duck at the dinner table… well all the better.

Wild Duck Meatballs

Serves 4

People who do not eat duck become duck lovers after eating these tasty meatballs. They are perfect for snacking or as a meal served over short grained sticky rice or Chinese noodles.

Pancetta adds flavor and keeps the meatballs from drying out.

Ingredients

2 tablespoons of olive oil plus more for sautéing
1 medium yellow onion, minced
1 pear, peeled and finely chopped
2 teaspoons ginger, minced
2 cloves garlic, minced
2 pounds duck meat, cubed
½ pound pancetta
½ tablespoon kosher salt
1 teaspoon fresh thyme
1 teaspoon fresh rosemary, chopped
½ teaspoon Dijon mustard
½ teaspoon red pepper flakes
½ teaspoon cumin
½ teaspoon pepper
¼ cup parsley

Heat olive oil in a 10 to 12 inch sauté pan. Add onions, pears, ginger, and garlic until completely caramelized and liquid has evaporated. Chill for about an hour.

In a medium bowl, combine duck and pancetta along with the remaining ingredients. Chill for an hour.

Mix all ingredients together. Feed ingredients through a meat grinder with the medium dye attachment.

Form 2 ounces ball from the meat mixture.

Heat 1 teaspoon olive oil in cast iron skillet until hot, but not smoking. Brown meatballs in batches. Cook until done all the way through, about 7 minutes.

Deglaze the pan with white wine. Season to taste and pour over meatballs.

Sprinkle parsley over the top of meatballs. Serve with wild rice, mashed potatoes, creamed spinach, pasta, or orzo. Honey or your favorite barbeque sauce complements it nicely.

The fancy word for this dish is Confit. It means to simply poach the meat in oil. Surprisingly, this dish is not at all greasy. This technique traps the juices in, reducing the possibility of tough or dry meat. Traditionally chefs only use the dark meat of the duck, but for this tasty sandwich, it works perfectly. It is super easy and extra flavorful.

You can treat just about any protein in this manner. Poaching duck and vegetables in oil until cooked through and then storing the meat covered in its fat was a traditional way of preservation.

Duck Hoagie *with* Chipotle Sauce *and* Cucumber Carrot Slaw

Serves 4

Ingredients

2 duck breasts
3 tablespoons Kosher salt
1 teaspoon pepper
1 teaspoon brown sugar
1 teaspoon cinnamon
½ teaspoon cayenne pepper
4-5 sprigs fresh rosemary
3 garlic cloves
olive oil, enough to cover duck breasts
Cucumber Carrot Slaw
Chipotle Mayonnaise
4 ciabatta rolls

Preheat oven to 225 degrees.

Season both sides of the duck breasts with salt, pepper, brown sugar, cinnamon and cayenne pepper and place breasts in a casserole dish just large enough to fit the duck. Place rosemary sprigs and garlic cloves in the casserole dish. Cover the duck with olive oil; Cover the pan with foil and cook for about 4-6 hours until tender.

Remove duck from casserole and place in a cast iron skillet over high heat. Sear both sides of the duck. Remove duck from skillet shred with a fork.

Slice ciabatta bread in half and spread Chipotle Mayonnaise (page 80) on bottom of 1 roll. Place slaw over the mayonnaise and top with shredded duck and top bun. Serve with Sweet Potato Fries.

Cucumber Carrot Slaw Ingredients

2 medium sized cucumbers
2 carrots
1 medium-sized Vidalia onion, thinly sliced
2 cups apple cider vinegar
1 lemon, juiced
½ teaspoon kosher salt
¼ teaspoon pepper

Peel cucumber and carrots with a vegetable peeler into long, thin strips and place in a medium-sized bowl. Add sliced onions to bowl.

In a separate bowl mix vinegar, lemon juice, salt and pepper. Pour over vegetables and marinade in refrigerator for at least 2 hours.

Quail

Quail is a small bird that is native to north America, though many many not know it due to its recent decline. Quail are a species of the edge. As large farms started overtaking the small family owned farms, there became less desirable habitat for the quail. Quail enjoy open woods, fields, and native grasses. Many of the corporate farms have miles of open expanses. Quail, being ground-dwellers, are also subject to their natural predators: cats, skunks, fox, raccoons, owls, snakes, dogs, and fire ants. The life span of quail is less than one year and the chicks have a 30% mortality rate. There are many organizations dedicated to preserving wild quail such as Quail Unlimited and Quail Forever.

If you do not have access to hunt wild quail, there are many high-end supermarkets that carry them in the freezer section. Quail are incredibly flavorful and are worthy of becoming one of your staple foods. They are small and therefore cook quickly making meals with quail great for entertaining or just a quick easy meal for your family.

I am hoping that quail will begin to populate the United States quickly. Many hunters are inadvertently enhancing quail habitat by managing their land for deer and turkey. We have personally seen an increase of quail on our managed farm in the past 5 years and are continuing to create better habitat for the quail.

Step 1 With the bird facing up, cut down each side of the backbone with kitchen scissors.

How to debone a quail

Step 2 Remove the wishbone by reaching into the neck cavity, massaging around the wishbone and pulling it out.

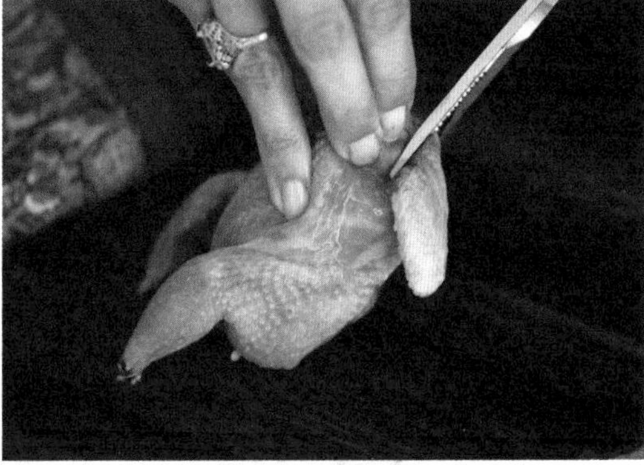

Step 3 With kitchen scissors, cut the wing joint (shoulder) to disconnect from ribcage.

Step 4 Remove ribcage by massaging the meat from the ribs. Be careful near the sternum because there is very little meat and it is only held together with skin. If recipe calls for a semi-deboned quail, this would be your last step.

Step 5 Massage meat away from leg bones as in step 4. Wings are left for presentation.

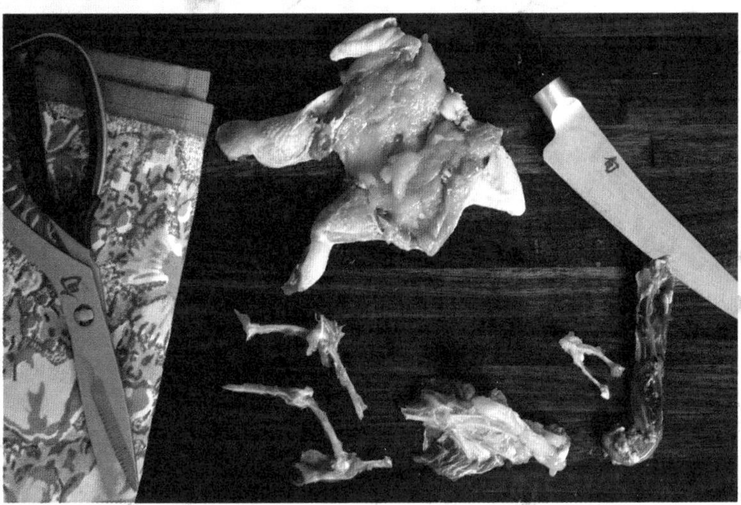

The creaminess of the grits and beans pair beautifully with the sweet figs, salty prosciutto, and rosemary infused quail. This meal is a true Southern delight that you will desire time and again.

Ingredients

4 boneless Quail
16 figs, divided
¼ pound prosciutto, chopped
4 sprigs rosemary 4 inches long
Parmesan Grits (page 165)
Kosher salt
Freshly ground pepper
Olive oil for browning and grilling
2 cups white beans, cooked and seasoned

Stuffed Quail with Figs and Prosciutto

Serves 4

Preheat oven to 375 degrees.

Begin preparing grits and warming beans.

Chop 12 figs and place in a bowl with chopped prosciutto. Combine and set aside.

Season each quail with salt and pepper. Lay quail skin side down on a plate or cutting board. Place fig and prosciutto stuffing in the center of the quail and wrap quail around the stuffing and secure with a rosemary sprig.

Heat olive oil in a cast iron skillet over high heat until almost smoking. Place quail breasts side down for about three minutes or until brown. Turn over and cook another 3 minutes.

Meanwhile heat grill over high heat. Slice remaining figs lengthwise and place flesh side down on grill for about 2 minutes. Remove from grill and set aside.

Place skillet into oven and cook quail for three to five minutes. Remove quail from oven.

Ladle about ½ cups of grits into four plates. Place the quail on the grits and serve with beans and grilled figs.

My very first hunting trip was spent with my husband on the most beautiful land in the middle of Nowhere, Alabama. Scott, my husband, and I were dating at the time, and his dog was finding quail like crazy. The hunt was an event like I had never seen before.

In-between the flushing of the birds, we were talking, eating, and enjoying the beautiful day. I had no idea you could talk while hunting. That made all the difference in the world to me about my decision to "like" hunting.

Besides the fantastic relationships that are built, quail hunting provide mighty amazing meals for the table. Quail's sweet tender meat is one of life's treasures. It seems through the years I have used quail in just about every way possible.

One of my favorite recipes, Rustic Quail Pizza, is among the tastiest preparations of quail and everyone I have ever fed this pizza is instantly won by its perfect flavor. Quail is so mild that it can taste bland, so the pizza's herbs and cheeses add just the perfect amount of everything bringing out the taste of the bird.

The dough can be made ahead and frozen. No worries if you don't have all of the ingredients. As long as the dough and sauce are right, you're good-to-go! Everything else is just "gravy."

Rustic Quail Pizza

Makes 2 Pizzas

Ingredients

8 cups self-rising flour, extra for dusting
1 tablespoon Kosher salt
1 tablespoon active dry yeast
2 ¾ cups warm water

Topping

1 pint crushed tomatoes
4 cloves garlic, minced
Juice of one lime
Tablespoon of thyme
½ cup of olive oil, for browning and sautéing
1 medium eggplant, skin removed and thinly sliced
4 green tomatoes, thinly sliced
1 pound mushrooms
1 cup cherry tomatoes, halved
Meat of 4 Pan Fried Quail (page 260)
1 pound prosciutto, sliced
1 pound sausage, browned
1 pound provolone, sliced
½ cup basil, chopped
Kosher salt to taste
2 ½ cups Parmesan cheese

Preheat oven to 400 degrees.

In a medium sized bowl, mix flour and salt. Sprinkle yeast over flour and slowly begin to incorporate warm water into the flour with clean hands or a wooden spoon. Using all of the water may not be necessary. Place dough in a non-humid location and let rest for 30 minutes.

Meanwhile, place crushed tomatoes, garlic, lime juice and thyme in a medium sized bowl and puree with a stick blender. If you do not have a stick blender place all ingredients in a food processor and puree.

Heat 2 tablespoons of olive oil in a large sauté pan. When oil is simmering add vegetables in batches until vegetables are soft.

Sprinkle flour onto work surface and place dough onto the floured surface. Split dough into two equal parts with a knife or a dough scraper. Starting from the center roll out one of the dough balls into a ⅛ inch thick rectangle. If dough is too sticky, sprinkle a little flour on dough and continue to roll. Place dough on a cookie sheet. Repeat with other dough ball.

Divide toppings between the two pizzas by first adding the sauce leaving an inch around the sides. Continue layering each pizza with the vegetables, meat of the Pan Fried Quail, provolone, prosciutto, and sausage. Lightly sprinkle entire pizza with salt including the edges. Sprinkle basil and Parmesan cheese evenly over pizzas.

Bake pizzas for 35 minutes or until golden brown and cheese is bubbly. Serve immediately.

Pan Fried Quail

Serves 4

If you want a quick meal full of flavor, this is the meal for you. It takes only minutes to caramelize the spicy sweet quail and have it over salad greens, sweet potatoes, or grits and satisfy your most ravenous cravings.

Ingredients

8 quail, deboned
¼ cup olive oil for browning
2 tablespoons cumin
1 tablespoon freshly ground pepper
½ teaspoon red pepper flakes
½ teaspoon cayenne pepper
2 tablespoons honey
½ teaspoon salt

In a medium sized bowl, mix all ingredients. Place quail in marinade for about 5 minutes.

Drizzle olive oil into a super hot skillet. When olive oil is shimmering, place quail in skillet for 3 minutes. Turn over and cook the other side for about 2 minutes. Remove the quail from the skillet and serve with Mashed Sweet Potatoes (page 83).

Small Game, Big Flavor

Fried Rabbit *and* Sage Buttermilk Waffles

Serves 4

Waffles and fried rabbit have been a tradition in my household as long as I can remember. Every one of my favorite foods is contained in this one mouthwatering dish!

Ingredients

1 rabbit, quartered and deboned
1 cup buttermilk
2 cups all-purpose flour
1 ½ tablespoons paprika
1 teaspoon kosher salt
½ teaspoon freshly ground pepper
Tabasco
3 cups of vegetable oil for frying
Sage Buttermilk Waffles (page 267)
Honey Butter (page 151)

Debone rabbit and soak in buttermilk overnight in a baking dish or zip top bag.

Combine flour, paprika, salt and pepper in a shallow dish.

Place a wire rack on a baking sheet and set aside.

Remove rabbit and discard buttermilk. Season rabbit with a few shakes of Tabasco. Dredge rabbit in flour mixture.

Pour oil in skillet to a depth of about ¾ inch. Oil should reach 350 degrees. Fry the rabbit in batches about 5 minutes on one side then turn and fry for 3-4 minutes on the other side. Move the rabbit to the wire rack on the cookie sheet and let rest. To keep warm while making the waffles place in a 200- degree oven. Serve with Sage Waffles, Honey Butter, and Maple syrup.

Sage Buttermilk Waffles

1 ¾ Cups flour
3 tablespoons sugar
3 tablespoons yellow cornmeal
½ teaspoon baking soda
½ teaspoon salt
2 cups buttermilk
1 tablespoon sage
2 tablespoons Dijon mustard
2 eggs
8 tablespoons Butter, melted

In a medium-sized bowl, combine flour, sugar, cornmeal, baking soda, and salt.

In another medium-sized bowl, whisk buttermilk, sage, mustard, and eggs.

Add wet ingredients into the dry ingredients and whisk melted butter into mixture.

Heat an oiled waffle iron and pour batter onto the griddle. Cook until crisped and golden brown. You will know it is ready when steam stops releasing from your waffle iron. Transfer the waffles to a serving plate and repeat with remaining batter. To keep waffles warm, place them in a 200 degree oven until ready to use.

I've heard that squirrel is just about the most ethical dishes you can serve on a dinner plate; it's free-range, plentiful, low in fat, and low in food miles (local). I know that there are a larger number of folks eating squirrel...it's got quite a nice flavor. Squirrel tastes sweet and is a good cross between duck and lamb.

Most kids get their first taste when squirrel hunting. I know the rule for my husband's home, and now our home, is that you eat what you harvest. Here's one of my favorite recipes to use with that first squirrel harvest of the year.

Southern Squirrel Pot Pie

Serves 4–6

Ingredients

1 ½ pounds squirrel meat, diced into ½ inch pieces
1 tablespoon all-purpose flour
2 tablespoon olive oil
1 large onion, diced
3 stalks celery, diced
2 carrots, peeled and diced
5 cloves garlic, minced
2 cups beef broth
2 cups Guinness (beer)
1 16 ounce can chopped tomatoes
3 sprigs fresh rosemary (1 tablespoon), finely chopped
4 sprigs thyme (2 tablespoons), finely chopped
1 handful flat-leaf parsley leaves (about ¼ cup), chopped
1 tablespoon Kosher salt
1 ½ teaspoons freshly ground pepper
1 pie crust (page 43)
1 large egg mixed with a teaspoon of water

Preheat oven to 400 degrees. In a medium sized bowl, toss the meat with the flour to coat.

In a large Dutch oven or heavy-bottomed pot, heat oil over medium-high heat until almost smoking. Working in batches, brown the meat on all sides until lightly browned and allow it to drain on a paper towel. Add more oil to the pan as you need it for optimal browning.

Add the onions, celery, and carrots and cook for about 5 minutes or until they are translucent and soft. Add the garlic and cook about 2 minutes more. Return the meat to the pan, then add the broth, Guinness, tomatoes, herbs, salt and pepper and allow to reach a boil. Scrape the bottom of the Dutch oven to loosen the brown bits and reduce the heat to simmer leaving the mixture uncovered for an hour or until it has thickened.

Pour mixture into a 9 inch pie dish and allow to cool completely. Brush the outer edges of the pie dish with melted butter and gently place the pie shell over the mixture pinching the edges to seal. Brush the egg and water mixture over the pie crust to enhance browning. Transfer the pie into the oven for about 30 to 40 minutes or until the crust is baked through and browned. Serve immediately with rice and a salad.

Seafood and Fish, Need I Say More?

Our family enjoys every kind of fishing, but especially deep sea fishing. We try to go on a deep sea fishing trip at least once yearly, with grandparents and friends. It is such fun to see the catch when they return to shore. Everyone usually has enough healthy fish to last until the next opportunity to go again.

We have many lakes and creeks around our community to catch bass, bream, catfish, and crappie. We love to canoe down the creek on our land and fly fish for red-eye bass and bream. We also love to canoe to the Coosa River and spend the day catching white bass. The kids also love a diversion from studying by going fishing with my dad to his favorite fishing hole "where the water is crystal clear."

Doctors and nutritionists around the world recommend that we eat a diet containing at least two servings of fish a week. Seafood is the favored choice because of its health benefits. Seafood is an excellent source of protein, is low in calories, low in saturated fat and cholesterol, high in polyunsaturated fat and Omega 3 fatty acids as well as packed full of vitamins and minerals. Most fish dishes are easy to make and can be prepared in as little as 15 minutes. There are many medical studies available that associated lower heart disease, diabetes and cancer with a diet that consumes 7 ounces of fish once per week.

There is, however, a difference in farm raised fish as opposed to naturally caught fish. When fishing from a lake or natural source for fish, the fish eat the plankton and other fishes found in the water. Whereas, farm raised fish are often fed additives to make them grow faster and diets formulated in granaries that are high in preservatives, glutens and corn products and by products. (Warning- be sure to purchase your seafood and/or fish from a reputable market place. Also, when fishing rivers and lakes, that these sources have not been polluted by chemicals expelled from various manufacturing companies).

FLOYD'S

Greek Snapper

Serves 6

This dish is incredibly easy to make, but is packed full of flavor. You could substitute any white flaky fish with the snapper and make the dish a weekly staple.

Ingredients

2 -3 tablespoons olive oil
2 pounds fresh snapper (about 2 large fillets)
½ teaspoon salt
¼ teaspoon pepper
½ Vidalia onion, chopped
½ cup Kalamatta olives
3 tablespoons capers
1 tablespoon garlic, minced
1 tablespoon fresh rosemary, chopped
1 pint (1 can) canned tomatoes
½ cup dry white wine

Preheat oven to 200 degrees.

Drizzle about a 2 tablespoon of olive oil in a large sauté pan over medium-high heat. Salt and pepper fillets and place in pan when oil is shimmering. Cook for 5 minutes and then turn fillets over and cook for another 3-5 minutes or until fish flakes easily. Place gently into a cookie sheet and place into oven with door cracked to keep warm.

Add remaining olive oil to pan. Sauté onions, olives, capers, garlic, and rosemary for about 5 minutes. Add tomatoes and wine to the medley and reduce for 5- 10 more minutes.

Remove snapper from oven, place on platter, and pour olive mixture over the fish. Serve with a side salad and a crusty bread.

Herb Pecan Crusted Trout

Serves 4

This dish is great for easy entertaining. The flavor of the trout is so mild that even the pickiest eaters will love it.

Ingredients

¾ cups pecans, finely chopped
2 tablespoons rosemary, finely chopped
¼ cup fresh parsley, finely chopped and divided
½ teaspoon salt
½ teaspoon pepper
1½ tablespoons Dijon mustard
4 6-ounce trout fillets, skinned
olive oil, for browning
2 tablespoons butter, plus more for browning
1 lemon, juiced
¼ cup white wine
3 tablespoons capers
2 cups spinach
2 cups arugula

On a plate, combine pecans, rosemary, half the parsley, salt and pepper.

Lightly brush one side of fillet with Dijon mustard and press fillet into the pecan mixture to adhere. Set aside and proceed with remaining fillets.

Heat about 1 tablespoon each of olive oil and butter over medium-high heat. When oil is sizzling hot, place fillets pecan-batter side down in pan and cook for about 3 minutes. Do not crowd the pan; you might have to cook in batches. Flip fillets and cook for about 2 more minutes, or until flaky and golden. Remove fillets to platter and tent with foil. Repeat with remaining fillets.

Once all fillets are cooked, add the butter, lemon juice, and wine to deglaze the pan. The brown bits from the fish are truly golden nuggets to be cherished! Add capers and bring to a boil. Turn off heat and stir in rest of parsley.

Prepare plates with spinach and arugula and top each one with a fillet. Divide wine sauce evenly among the plates and serve immediately.

Best Ever Clam Bake

Serves 8

We recently celebrated 2 birthdays on the same day and no they are not twins. My oldest son and my oldest daughter are 5 years apart. On every birthday each child gets to choose his or her favorite meal and dessert. At least 4 out of 7 birthdays we will have our famous clambake. The seafood is incredibly beautiful and it looks as if it took hours to prepare, but in reality it only takes about 30 minutes to make. Not only is this dish tasty and beautiful, the clean up time is minimal as well! How great is that?

Splitting the lobster lengthwise down the middle of the tails underside keeps the tail from curling during cooking.

Ingredients

½ cup olive oil
2 large onions, chopped
6 cloves garlic
2 pounds red potatoes
2 pounds kielbasa, sliced 1" thick diagonally
1 tablespoon salt
½ tablespoon freshly ground pepper
6 sprigs thyme
3 cups good white wine
1 cup fish stock
6 ears of corn, husked and snapped in half
3 dozen little neck clams, scrubbed
1 lobster tail, split lengthwise down the flesh
1 ½ pounds large shrimp, deveined and in the shell
2 pounds mussels, de-bearded and cleaned
3 tablespoons butter

In a 20 quart pot, sauté onions in olive oil for 15 minutes or until onions start to brown. Put garlic into pot and cook for 2 more minutes.

Place potatoes, kielbasa, salt, pepper, and thyme on top of the onions and pour in the white wine and fish stock. Cover with a lid and cook medium high heat for 20 minutes.

Place corn, clams, and lobster into pot for 5 minutes. Covering the pot tightly.

Add the shrimp and mussels to the pot for 5 minutes. Test the potatoes for tenderness. The lobster and shrimp should be opaque and the clams and mussels should be opened. If not cook a few more minutes. With a large slotted spoon, remove the vegetables and seafood to a large bowl. Add 3 tablespoons of butter to the broth and bring to a boil. Season to taste. Serve over the clambake. Serve with crusty bread.

Fish Tacos

Serves 4–6

Ingredients

2 cups Vidalia onions, chopped
½ cup fresh cilantro
2 cloves garlic, minced
2 teaspoons oregano
½ teaspoon salt
⅓ cup olive oil
¼ cup lime juice, plus wedges of lime for garnish
4 scamp fillet
12 small flour tortillas
Lime mayonnaise
3 avocados, sliced
Pica de Gallo (page 220)

In a medium bowl, mix onions, cilantro, garlic, oregano, salt, oil, and lime juice. Pour half the mixture into a 9"x11" casserole. Place fish fillets on top of mixture. Pour the remaining marinade over fish. Cover and chill for 1 hour.

Heat griddle on grill to almost smoking. Place fillets on hot grill for 2–3 minutes. Turn and cook for another 2–3 minutes or until fish is opaque. Remove from heat and set aside.

Grill tortillas for about 10 seconds per side.

Coarsely chop fish and place on tortilla. Drizzle lime mayonnaise on top of fish and place avocado and Pica de Gallo on top. Serve with lime wedges.

LIME MAYONNAISE

If you need a shortcut use mayonnaise and mix with lime juice.

All ingredients must be at room temperature.

Ingredients

1 egg
2 egg yolks
2 tablespoons lime juice
1 teaspoon Dijon mustard
½ teaspoon salt
Dash of Tabasco sauce
2 cups olive oil

In a food processor, add; egg, egg yolks, lime juice, mustard, salt, and Tabasco sauce.

Start food processor and run continually while very slowly adding drops off oil, waiting 10 seconds between each drop. Continue with the drops for about ¼ cup of oil.

When mayonnaise has definitely thickened, add oil in a stream. You may not need all the oil at this time, therefore, check after each ½ cup is added for thickness and taste. If the consistency is very thick, add a drop of lime to thin it or if too thin add more oil.

Place mayonnaise in a bowl and serve or keep covered in refrigerator for 1 week.

Fish tacos are one of our family's favorite summer time staples. After a day of fishing, we come home, pick fresh herbs and sit out on the porch eating this scrumptious treat making great memories.

Side note: You can substitute any white flaky fish for this recipe.

Crappie *with* White Beans *and* Basil

Serves 4 to 6

Creamy beans and Crappie is the ultimate fish comfort food. The creaminess of the beans with the flakiness of the fish and a few shakes of Tabasco is to me the perfect fish dish. While eating this mild, white, flaky fish, I am reminded that summer is just around the corner.

If you are in a hurry, use canned cannellini or navy beans. Rinse the beans and add about ¼ cup water to the bean mixture in the recipe.

Ingredients

¾ cup white beans
6 crappie fillets
Kosher salt
Freshly ground black pepper
Olive oil for sautéing
1 teaspoon fresh basil plus, extra for garnish; chopped
1 teaspoon fresh parsley, plus extra for garnish; chopped
½ lemon, juiced

Place white beans in a medium pot with water covering beans 2 inches. Bring water to boil, then lower heat to a simmer for about 45 minutes.

Meanwhile, season crappie fillets liberally with salt and pepper.

Drizzle olive oil into a heated sauté pan. When oil is shimmering, place crappie in pan and cook for 3 minutes. Lower heat to medium. Turn over fillet and cook for another 2–3 minutes. Remove from heat and repeat with remaining fillets.

Add basil, parsley, and lemon juice to the beans and bring back to boil, and then lower to simmer.

Season beans with salt and divide among 6 shallow bowls. Top the beans with the crappie fillet. Garnish with remaining chopped basil and parsley, and a drizzle of olive oil.

Thanks!

One of my favorite things to do is to share tried and true recipes and tips for the sustainable lifestyle in a way that is fun and beautiful. Thankfully, I am surrounded with the most brilliant, talented, and creative people I have ever known. Working on a cookbook is not an individual endeavor, but quite a collaboration of many creative minds. I would like to thank those creative people who have poured their energy into developing exactly what I have envisioned.

First is my wonderful husband who encourages me in every enterprise I set my heart on accomplishing and for supporting me in every way possible. He is the creative mind that brings all my thoughts together in an amazing way. Second is my children: Hunter for helping me plan, research, and implement the garden; Hampton for video and editing work; Graylyn for helping with the photos, cooking, and listening to my ideas everyday; Howlett for keeping the yard, porches, and house in working order; Mary Elizabeth for keeping me organized, understanding what I need and doing what it takes to make it all work; Anna Julia for helping Mary run the house when I have deadlines, and Milly for making our house so happy.

They have all played a role in the making of this book from the planting, saving, harvesting of the seeds to the cooking of the recipes, cleaning the kitchen, and anything and everything asked of them. I could not ask for more in my children. They are my heart and inspiration for all my projects and are the delight of my life.

I would also like to thank my mom, Paula Johnson, who has supported me through the development of my books and my dad, Wayne Pilgreen, who is the inspiration for much of the book, my mother-in-law, Kay Harris, and father-in-law, Andy Harris for pouring out your prayers over my book endeavors.

A major thanks to Lynne Hopwood, a most talented designer whose belief in me never dies, and to Mel Cohen for benevolently providing his extensive and un-ending knowledge of publishing and assistance.

I could not have written this book without all of those listed. I also want to thank all of you who are reading this book for your support and for allowing me the privilege of being a part of your lives.

Subscribe to my website,
www.StacyLynHarris.com,
and get free recipes and special offers!
You will also find my books and our latest antique wood hand-hewn and hand-crafted platters, cutting boards, bowls, spoons, gumbo paddles, and more.
Each product is unique and made to last your lifetime and into future generations. Place your order today!

Index